Straight To Yes!

Asking with Confidence and Getting What You Want

Haider Imam

CAPSTONE

Registered office
Capstone Publishing Ltd. (A Wiley Company), John Wiley and Sons Ltd, The Atrium,
Southern Gate, Chichester, West Sussex, PO19 8SQ, United Kingdom.

For details of our global editorial offices, for customer services and for information about
how to apply for permission to reuse the copyright material in this book please see our
website at www.wiley.com.

Library of Congress Cataloging-in-Publication Data

Imam, Haider, 1972–
   Straight to yes! : asking with confidence and getting what you want / Haider Imam.
     p. cm.
   Includes bibliographical references and index.
   ISBN 978-0-85708-375-3 (pbk.)
   1. Persuasion (Psychology)   2. Persuasion (Psychology) in organizations. I. Title.
   BF637.P4I43 2013
   153.8'52–dc23
                                                    2012038295

A catalogue record for this book is available from the British Library.

ISBN 978-0-857-08375-3 (paperback)   ISBN 978-0-857-08376-0 (ebk)
ISBN 978-0-857-08378-4 (ebk)   ISBN 978-0-857-08377-7 (ebk)

Cover design: Binary & The Brain

Set in 10/13.5pt ACaslon Pro-Regular by Toppan Best-set Premedia Limited
Printed in Great Britain by TJ International Ltd, Padstow, Cornwall, UK

Dedicated to

Marie-Claire, La'ali and Omar – my beloved and inspirational tribe.

And to the thinkers of great thoughts: the world's greatest idea,
without someone saying, "Yes!" to it, is as nothing.
I sincerely hope this book unlocks possibilities,
recognition and reward for you.

Contents

Introduction: Why Getting "Straight to Yes!" is So
Relevant Today   1

1 Asking: The "Inner Game"   11
2 Getting Ready for the Ask   21

Part One – Asking with Frames in Mind   **33**
3 Consistency   37
4 Same and Different   49
5 Ready for Business   65
6 The Way We See It   79

Part Two – Asking with Tribes in Mind   **87**
7 Body Talk   91
8 The Name's Bond ... Social Bond   105
9 The Wider Tribe   119
10 Progressive Feedback Loops   133

Part Three – Asking with the Brain in Mind   **143**
11 The Loss and Pain Brain   147
12 Reactance   161
13 Pattern Breakers   169
14 Priming   179

Part Four – Commencement   **193**
15 Actively Reflect   195
16 Good Integrate!   199

17 Some Asks to Avoid   203
18 Making Sure It Sticks   207
3 ... 2 ... 1 ... Commence!   211

About the Author   213
Acknowledgements   215
References   217
Index   227

Introduction: Why Getting "Straight to Yes!" is So Relevant Today

There's an age-old Geordie saying from more austere times, which goes something like, "Shy bairns get nae broth," meaning "shy children don't get any soup." And it's becoming truer in modern life. We live in an age of unparalleled competition for resources. At the time of writing there are seven people competing for every one university degree place in the UK. There is record unemployment in many parts of Europe, leading to intense competition to hold onto jobs or secure promotions. More than 40,000,000 people are using online dating in the US, all competing for the same hearts. Across the world, famous brand name businesses have closed down their doors because of recession and insufficient sales to turn them around. Undeniably, these are challenging times.

So, congratulations! What you're in possession of and reading right now is undeniably an exciting and enticing prospect: the ability to fine-tune your game to make a measurable and noticeable impact with your target audience. The content contained within has been proven effective in multiple business models across multiple industries, cultures and continents. However, before we get into the main flow of the book, I'd like to offer some personalized thoughts for you on why this collection of short, simple, practical techniques is so relevant to you.

An Evolving Business Paradigm

Business leaders around the globe are struggling to cope with the break-neck pace of change in their markets and consumer buying patterns. Micro-financing, neuromarketing and social networking are just three examples of how our world is becoming more opportunistic, sophisticated and connected. Perhaps most challenging of all is the demise of authority as a main source of influence. Since the swinging '60s, attitudes to "authority figures" have been evolving rapidly. Now the ageing baby boomers that masterminded this shift are tasting the fruits of their labour courtesy of *Generation Y* (also known as *the Millennials*). Gen Y, as a generalization, attributes far less clout to rank and file than previous generations: it's a generation that wants to be enfranchised, included in the planning and wooed to join in. It likes autonomy and flat organizations. It likes Twitter and Facebook. It dislikes hierarchy and red tape. Its preference is to deliver change *through* people not *to* people.

Add to Gen Y the reality of a global labour market: a modern leader of a multinational corporation may contend with offices across the world and a call centre in Mumbai with contrasting cultural attitudes, but even the leaders of a small business may have a dozen different nationalities and cultures working in their very own office. Using the same old management, leadership and influence approaches from yesteryear with this new workforce demographic is a recipe for disaster. If we abuse them, we lose them, which will damage our results and our reputation. The fact is that in today's marketplace, job loyalty is rare. Many executives I know keep their details on job hunt sites or headhunters' lists because they're always looking for that next step up the career ladder. The crumbling paradigm of a "job for life" is rapidly being replaced by multiple careers, micro-businesses, joint ventures and an entrepreneurial revolution. Even some of the major organizations my company works with engage us specifically to help their leaders become more entrepreneurial. Losing good people is exactly what you don't need when you feel you're constantly under scrutiny, while attempting to deliver more with fewer resources.

An Increasing Need to Create Buy-In

As people in business, we're having to retain or attract increasingly switched-on customers, who've already researched five alternative options (with crowd-sourced reviews) on their mobile phones before our meeting. Because the purchase options are more numerous, more similar and often more confusing, gaining instant commitment to move our way has become noticeably less straightforward. Since the customer increasingly expects a degree of personalization and flexibility from us, we now have to negotiate and persuade *internally* more than ever – to get that discount, to make that exception, to add a new feature, to work as part of a supplier coalition . . .

As executives, project leaders or managers, we're often working in ever-flatter organizations, matrix teams or task forces where no single member of the group has more appointed authority than any other member. Often, each of us has what we see as the best idea in the meeting and our ego is bruised if others don't agree. We fight internal politics, cliques and silo thinking. We are obsessed with creating "buy-in" for our ideas, so that our ideas stick and bear fruit. It's certainly not easy. Added to that, we're ambitious. We want to do a great job and be seen to be doing so, in order to move up through the organization. We want to influence our bosses to buy into our ideas, to rate us more highly at review time, to give us a bigger salary increase.

But the greatest idea or most noble intent, championed by the poorest persuader will forever remain unheard.

A Fight for Resources

At the best of times, we have to work hard to gain sponsorship for our cause, be that in the form of time, money, public support or otherwise. Now, in an age of cutbacks, reductions in real earnings and record low disposable income, our organizations bravely face even more of a challenge: to persuade people in the toughest of times to spend or donate generously, with fewer resources to get in front of them.

A Challenge Closer to Home

As a child of the '70s, I grew up in an age of being present. I'd play with friends or by myself with twigs, ropes, cap guns and Lego; we'd spend an entire day riding our bikes around the countryside wearing our jackets as capes and our mudguards folded under to sound like a motorbike. We had computers, but played them infrequently. We had no Internet, no mobile phones. If anyone wanted to reach us, including our parents, they'd have to leave a message with someone and wait until we received it.

Nowadays our children are constantly "on," or at least want to be. If we're not vigilant, they'll watch TV while listening to music and researching their homework on a notebook, connected to a school virtual learning environment and interacting with friends via Facebook and Twitter. In some ways, they're more confident, more exposed to the world, more clued up. They study work in primary school that we studied in high school. They live, grow and think at a rate far faster than we did. We have fewer extended families in touch with each other and elders, the bedrock of society, don't have the same relevance: they were of use when life was predictable and came in cycles. From the perspective of many of our children, the rate of change nowadays weakens authority figures' credibility.

But they're still kids and they still need direction. Which is difficult when they're 13 years old and taller than us, thinking that we don't understand the way the world works nowadays. The more we direct and instruct, the more opposition we create.

Time: The New Currency

Arguably, there's something even more important than a shifting attitude to authority, flatter organizations and increased competition for resources – time. Studies show we are working longer hours, spending less time at home and even walking 10% faster than a decade ago. The amount of interactions we have on a weekly basis has increased exponentially, often meaning we have less time with each person to get something done. Isn't the ability to consistently get *straight to yes* with more people, bypassing long, drawn-out conversations but in a way that also promotes healthy relationships, something that we all need?

Contained within this book is a collection of the fastest ways to yes known to man. Simple methods that will boost your results *and* your relationships, enlist, persuade and motivate your audience – all designed for a new age of influence.

In Summary

Perhaps it's fair to say that modern-day possibilities match modern-day problems. It's the age of the entrepreneur. But entrepreneurship is not what we're taught at school. There are very few classes I know of that teach our children business thinking, pitching for funding, marketing, sales, consumer psychology or leadership. Certain schools offer enterprise schemes for selected children to give them some of this experience; some schools have connections with industry but, in reality, the numbers are negligible.

The bottom line is that we emerge into a new world, lacking the basic skills that we'll need during the course of our natural working life. Uplifting, eh?

So, you have some choices here. You can:

1. Write a letter to your old head teacher or principal, explaining in detail how they failed to prepare you for the "Information and Persuasion Age."
2. Write a letter to your children's head teacher or principal, asking why these skills are not in their curriculum or extra-curricular activities.

"

I was working for a leading building society when my marriage broke up. It was agreed that my departing husband would sign the property over to me together with his debts. However, my salary at the time clearly wouldn't cover the repayments let alone leave me with enough to live on. I had to find an additional source of income *and I had to make my employers believe it benefitted them* to let me take the mortgage on my own. But at the time the company had a policy of not permitting staff to "double job."

Once I had a plan to cover my costs I went to my line manager, who said she couldn't help and referred me to the branch manager. The branch manager said it was out of the question, so I asked to be referred to the regional manager to outline my plan, who after meeting with me agreed to recommend my case to Head Office and, with certain provisos, they agreed!

I got a huge amount of job satisfaction for the next few years. I worked with the branch team consistently achieving best results in both the region and the county league tables, never took a day off sick and never went into arrears with my mortgage payments. I paid off my debts and vastly reduced the outstanding mortgage, which later gave me and my new partner the opportunity to buy our dream home.

Within ten years of buying the property, we'd paid off our mortgage completely. All because I asked.

By Margaret Ginnelly, 50-something graduate of the University of Life, currently volunteering and supporting her partner's business www.needonesoon.com

"

3. Realize that teachers are angels, working in a system that mandates what and how they teach and are doing the best job they can with limited resources in a world that's changing so fast that no one really knows what to expect in five years' time, let alone 15, meaning that it's time for you to take action yourself.

If your choice included option 3, this book may serve you well.

Suggestions on How Best to Use This Book

Learning should always be an enjoyable thing! One thing we know from neuroscientific research is that learning is dependent on the emotional state you're in while you're learning it.

So, to quote a mentor of mine, if you want to feel stressed when putting the learning into practice, feel stressed while learning it! If you want to feel playful, confident and energized when using the learning, feel playful, confident and energized while learning it.

Take your time with it. This book is not a novel. It's not designed to be read from cover to cover in one sitting. It is, however, full to bursting with ripe and juicy standalone techniques that may seduce you into trying them out. Read one, practise one. Read some more, practise some more. Remember, it's a myth that practice makes perfect; *perfect* practice makes perfect. If you practise the learning in a rushed, incorrect and half-hearted fashion, you're creating neural connections that make it more likely you'll repeat it incorrectly next time you try. Don't expect to go from riding with stabilizers to "popping a wheelie" by the end of this book. Expecting a life-changing breakthrough often gets in the way of real, lasting change. If you can be disciplined enough, I'd suggest trying one or two per week and seeing which ones work for you before trying another. Imagine if you hadn't exercised for years and then rushed into the gym for three days straight, lifting every single weight and trying out every single machine. You'd end up in hospital. Go easy and go gently.

This book is written with face-to-face communicating in mind but many of the strategies in this book will work equally well with online marketing and emails. When communicating, nothing is as rich, satisfying and productive as a face-to-face interaction, so whenever possible, make the effort to meet up. However, look out for certain techniques within this book that are exclusively relevant to the written word.

After each technique, I've suggested some practical ways in which you can immediately "try it." These are suggestions based on my experience of what works; I'd encourage you to have a go but also to create your own nuances, based on the theory – just ask yourself, "How else might I use this?"

I'll also point out two other interesting features of *Straight to Yes!* As I began this book, I considered ways in which I might add a few extra spoonfuls of added value. So, as you progress through the book, you'll notice that certain exclusive online resources become available to support your success, with my compliments. Just follow the steps to download them.

Second, throughout this book you'll encounter personal thoughts and stories from a collection of highly successful influencers. Some are leaders of well-known international brands, with responsibility to thousands of employees; some are children. Most were known to me at the outset; some I approached after they were heartily recommended by my network. What they all have in common is an uncanny ability to influence people ethically, inspire action and get results. Each story outlines the contributor's favourite way of getting "Straight to Yes!" or their thoughts about the importance of being able to inspire people to action. I enjoyed the process of asking for them as much as I appreciated the decades of wisdom emanating from each story. I hope you enjoy them, too.

Ethics and the Beautiful Dark Side

The material in this book is powerful and controversial. It's responsible for some huge increases in success for my private and corporate clients. It can be used for profit or "not-for-profit," for good or for "not good." It's worth noting that no single strategy, technique or behaviour is good or bad – it's only the context and the intent of the practitioner that makes it so. The line demarcating a positive ethic from a negative one is yours and yours alone to decide. Please choose wisely and pro-socially.

I'd also like to add a note about the "beautiful dark side" of asking. As you'll discover, there's a powerful psychological concept at large in the world, called "reciprocity." In essence, it means that when someone gives us something or does us a favour, we become more inclined to "reciprocate" it; in other words, giving them something of equal value or greater back in return.

In short, the more you get from asking, the more you may become obligated to those who give to you. Fear not, it's healthy and desirable! It's how we form durable communities, relationships and economies. I just want you to be prepared for the journey ahead, so that you ask the right people for the right things. In other words, don't ask a notorious gangster for a huge favour: they just might demand it back, in kind.

My favourite method of persuasion is repeated asking. This has proved to be useful when asking for many things, yet it was arguably the most useful when I was asking for a dog.

It all started when we were in Ireland and met a dog while walking along a path in the countryside. It followed us a long way down the road before stopping and refusing to move another inch. Though my parents tried to convince me that getting a dog was a bad idea, there was no stopping me once I got my mind on something.

I asked for my dog for about eight weeks (until my birthday) and kept on adding new reasons why I should get the dog, like, "it will help me to be more responsible" and "I won't pester people and annoy them because I'll have something to do." Finally, on the day before my birthday, my parents crumbled and found an awesome rescue dog only forty minutes away. Repeated asking can take a long time but it is normally worth it.

By Omar Imam-Gutierrez, age 12

CHAPTER 1
Asking: The "Inner Game"

You Were Born to Ask

You were born to ask. It's your natural way of being. Think about it: have you ever noticed that children ask for anything and everything with no shame? They ask as if they expect to get it and if they don't, they ask again and then ask someone else. They're annoyingly persistent sometimes. And they have a million and one creative ways of getting you to finally say, "Yes."

Here's the problem. As they get older, we erase this natural skill from their make-up by saying things such as, "Stop asking, it's annoying," "Don't be cheeky," "Don't be greedy," "It's rude to ask for that," "You don't hear other people asking all the time, do you?" or just a definitive "No!" in answer to each outlandish request.

I've even seen embarrassed British parents pull their child's eagerly outstretched arm down when the group of little ones was asked, "Who'd like a chocolate biscuit?" at a fête.

We mean to teach them patience, social norms, moderation, not to be needy or greedy and appreciate the value of things, but what we really do is to plant the messages, "It's not good to ask all the time" and "Asking for stuff from strangers is socially unacceptable."

Here, in the 21st century, both premises are wrong. So, you have some choices here. You can:

1. Go and rant about it to your parents – it's all their fault anyway.
2. Find a Gestalt therapist, imagine your parents are sitting on the two empty chairs next to you and rant about it to them – it's all their fault anyway.
3. Realize that it was a well-intentioned but anachronistic hand-me-down, start encouraging the opposite behaviour in your kids and start re-learning how to ask. It's all there, deep down . . .

If you chose option 3, congratulations, you're ready for the next section!

Naturally "X" People

Until recently, one of the greatest debates alive was "nature vs. nurture." It was a term coined by an English polymath from the Victorian era, Francis Galton, the cousin of Charles Darwin.

In our context, advocates of the "nature" standpoint would argue for heredity: that some people are just born influential, confident, charismatic, bold, fearless, playful – it's in their DNA. They'd quote various experiments with separated identical twins around the world, who are reunited only to find that they have had the same career, wear the same clothes and married almost identical spouses. Fascinating and scary – if you Google "Eugenics" you'll discover the dark side of this standpoint.

Advocates of the "nurture" standpoint would argue for environment: that people are a product of the social, physical, geographical and political conditions in which they grow up. A young girl growing up in 16th century China would have a very different personality, brain function and life to a young girl growing up in 21st century San Francisco, for example.

The arguments on each side are solid, compelling and convincing. But leading geneticists and psychologists such as Steve Jones, head of the Department of Genetics, Evolution and Environment at

University College London, and Jerome Kagan, Emeritus Professor of Psychology at Harvard University, both declare the argument as misguided in a modern-day context.

For example, the possession of the gene variant that disrupts serotonin activity in the brain can result in social anxiety in a woman raised in a stable middle-class family. But it can contribute to criminal behaviour in a man brought up in poverty by abusive parents.

While we do know that physically attractive people are *attributed* positive traits by others, isolating nature from nurture is like trying to separate salt from the stew after you've added it – it's futile and rather impossible. We are all a product of both. And without wanting to freak you out too much, did you know that having powerful new emotional experiences actually activates new DNA within your system? So it's not just about the fact that it's in our DNA, but rather what elements of our DNA are awoken by our experiences![1]

So, what do you think now about people who you used to think were naturally confident, charming, influential and so on? If you still think you don't naturally possess one or all of those desired traits, how do you know that it's not just because of the environmental factors so far in your life?

Because it is; and once you practise and get some positive feedback, your confidence will flourish. By investing your time in practising the contents of this book, you're boosting the environmental factors needed to adopt those traits as your own.

So, some choices at this stage. After choosing, you might like to take a break from reading: "heavy" information takes a lot of glucose from the brain, which you'll need to replace to optimize your learning.

1. Carry on thinking that people were born confident, intelligent, able and successful because of their DNA and wonder what would have happened if your mother had mixed her genes with a male super model, world champion martial artist with an MBA from Harvard and a penchant for climbing K2 for fun.

2. Carry on thinking that you didn't have "the right" conditions growing up and wonder what would have happened if you'd had a rich, stable family, access to influential people, a ready-made network of successful folk with open doors, the right name, colour, race, religion, school, university or neighbourhood.
3. Take to heart that anyone can learn a new skill to a high level and develop new traits given the right motivation, instruction, support, attitude and time.

If you plumped for option 3, you're in for some pretty major rewards from this book.

The Inhibitors

This book isn't a therapy book. Nor is it a life-coaching book. I'm making no promise to transform your confidence, body, career, wealth or love life! (If that's your goal, I recommend books or audio programmes by the wonderful Michael Neill or Paul McKenna.) It's not so much a book about the "inner game" of asking, as it is a practical handbook of strategies, knowledge and approaches. That said, I want to spend a few moments with you bringing your awareness to some of the inner hurdles that people sometimes have to rise above, at key points in their journey. Forewarned is forearmed, as they say, and I genuinely believe that we're all very similar in our barriers to success.

Over the last five years I've been blessed and focused enough to have trained or coached thousands of people from different cultures, backgrounds, industries and abilities. Some have been CEOs with thousands of people reporting to them and a board on their back; others have been entrepreneurs flying solo. Regardless of the face or the place, I've noticed that the same five inhibitors tend to pop up again and again. If you're prepared for these insidious inhibitors, my guess is you'll gain far more control and flexibility in response should you encounter them.

Issue #1: deserving

Question: When you say to yourself, "I deserve everything that life has to offer in abundance: vibrant health, incredible friends, supportive family, stupendous wealth, heavenly love, exciting travel, a fulfilling romantic life, daring adventure, ecstatic happiness, the power to change the planet and worldwide recognition for my gifts!" do you feel a resounding and convincing "YES!" coursing through your veins? Or do you feel a bit of a fake? If you came over a bit fakey, you very likely have a belief that you've been limiting yourself with – and it may well be around deserving or worthiness. "I'm not enough" is one of the greatest fears we all share in our dark moments.

I believe that the concept of deserving is . . . well, quite frankly, a bit weird. The wonderful writer and life coach, Mandy Evans, usually responds with the following three questions to an "I don't deserve it." As follows:

1. How do you know?
2. How could you find out?
3. Who's in charge of handing out deserving anyway?

I can't say it any better than her, so I suggest you watch her on YouTube. If you search "Deserving is a Bogus Issue with Mandy Evans" on YouTube,[2] you'll see that she's rather wonderful.

Issue #2: fear of rejection

Rejection and the fear of failure seldom make an explicit appearance in people's conversations, but they're often lurking there, implicitly. Like "deserving," rejection is also fairly hardcore. It stems from our need to be part of a tribe, pack or society because group size vastly increases our chances of finding food, protection, shelter, learning and mates.

As crazy as it sounds, being rejected makes us feel less secure within the group, which threatens our chances of survival. That could lead to starvation, having to fight off a saber-toothed tiger single-handedly, or dying a childless virgin. Is that a bit over the top? Of course it is. It's just someone saying, "No" to you! Get over it!

Great askers are also "No collectors." Why? Because they ask more often than anyone else and they ask bigger than anyone else. And somewhere in the flood of "no's" they receive, they hear the "yeses" popping out. In fact, if you're not getting plenty of "no's," you're doing something wrong: either not asking often enough or not asking big enough.

It's critical that you start to build your rejection muscle now. It gets easier to hear the "No" responses the more often you get them. Go for no. It also has an interesting positive side effect, explored in Chapter 4.

One interesting aside on the topic of rejection is that it goes both ways. Recent research shows that the act of rejection hurts the rejecter as well as the rejected: the act of rejecting reduces the desire to reconnect with anyone for a period of time after.[3] So, you can feel compassion for those who tell you "No." First, they're missing out on your great offer and second, saying "No" has a socio-emotional cost attached for them.

Issue #3: fear of success

Less common, though common enough to check out, is the fear of success, which I've witnessed on a few different levels. This was my own personal barrier. The first is a social level. When someone starts having a new level of success (in whatever way they personally define success) it can create unsettling ripples in their family and social groups. For example, some friends are intimidated by your newfound success – it changes the interpersonal dynamics of your relationship with them.

This can result in them asking themselves questions such as, "Do I feel comfortable around her now?," "Does he think less of me now he's so successful?" or even, "Who does he think he is? Is he too good for this (my) lifestyle now?" The spectre of rejection rises up in them and rather than be rejected, they voluntarily withdraw. On some level, we know that and sometimes it stops us from going for that new job, starting the business, finding a new and different-acting friend or peer group to hang out with. Faced with losing what we already have in order to gain something we don't yet have, we often go for not losing, a strategy you'll see in later chapters. "A bird in the hand is worth two in the bush . . ." as they say.

The second level is about your "blueprint" of life. Each of us designs, and lets others design for us, a plan for what life can be like: what we can experience, achieve and contribute. Most of us never think about proactively redesigning it. Unfortunately, most blueprints are a mish-mash of parental and peer group expectations and times where we've tried, failed and given up.

As soon as we start stepping off the blueprint, the extruder alarms start going off and that's enough for most people to return to the plan, as is. Because what would it mean if you stepped up your game and started living a more fulfilling life? Could you take the pressure of maintaining it? What would happen if it all disappeared? Would you feel truly deserving of the accolades, recognition and honour? What if you achieved enlightenment and still weren't happy?

Rather than dealing with these challenging questions, we self-sabotage and step back onto the blueprint, where we're safe. For a fleeting moment. Because, as leadership guru Seth Godin states, in today's world, not taking risks is itself the biggest risk of all.

I believe that you are the architect of your own experience and if you haven't got a plan, you're following someone else's. A good coach can help you with this part. If you haven't got one or can't afford one right now, I offer a free interactive coaching app for Windows or Mac at www.soinflow.com as a gift to you. You can go to "Free," then "Inspire" to download it. No adverts, no cost. It will walk you through a process to clarify your mission, vision and values as well as some next steps.

Issue #4: fear of discomfort

Often, when doing or preparing for field tasks, such as "Freedom shopping" (you'll find that in Chapter 4), my clients start getting cold feet; "It doesn't feel comfortable," is a common thing I hear. And that's both accurate and fine. As Henry Ford was heard to say, "If you do what you've always done, you'll get what you always got!" So, if you want something different, you have to do something differently.

Feeling discomfort means you're stepping outside your comfort zone. It doesn't always feel great, but it's good for you. And the only place where personal growth happens, by definition, is outside your comfort zone. Remember your growing pains as a child? What would have happened if your parents had given you drugs to stop the growth to stop the pain? You'd be "rather wee" as they say in Scotland!

So, that icky feeling just means you're getting ready to grow! Remember that and embrace it when it happens.

Issue #5: wrong peer group

There's an interesting and fairly accurate law that states, "Add the wages of the seven peers you most closely associate with. Divide by seven, to get an average. This figure is likely very close to your own earnings." Think about the anecdotes actors share, where it sounds like they're unable to hold onto names, dropping one every second; mentioning rock stars, actors and directors who they were at a party with. Who does Richard Branson invite to Necker Island, other than family and an employee or two? Kate Winslet, Janet Jackson, Harrison Ford, Mariah Carey, Eddie Murphy and Oprah Winfrey! How many unemployed people hang around with neurosurgeons and business owners? Now try replacing "wages" with earnings, happiness, health, weight, number of children, strength of marriage, qualifications and see what happens. It's an interesting exercise and usually pretty accurate.

The point is that millionaires tend to hang around with million-aires; jobless with jobless; artists with artists; habitually confident with habitually confident; shy and retiring with . . . well, with no one, of course! If you're looking to change your results, it's important to be associating closely and frequently with other people who are already achieving, or on the way to achieving, those results.

> "Your results in life are directly proportionate to the expectations of your peer group."
>
> **Tony Robbins, American success guru**

Read this quote a couple of times more and let it sink in. In today's world, your network and your network intelligence is where your real power lies.

So, choice time is here. You can:

1. Continue reading and treat the strategies in this book as "interesting information" but avoid trying them out in case your inhibitors kick in.
2. Continue reading and "flirt" with the ideas in this book, with no real commitment to making them work, in case your inhibitors kick in.
3. Continue reading and put the strategies into action, one at a time, knowing that some will work better than others for you, that perfect practice is the key and understanding that any discomfort that arises is purely a test to see how much you really want the prize you seek.

If you chose option 3, you're in the minority. But history repeatedly demonstrates that the rewards of the "slumbering many" go to "the daring few."

See you in the next section!

In June 2012, I lost a very dear friend. At the tender age of 42, Steve Brown's heart stopped. No warning, no illness, just stopped. In the days following this tragic event I discovered he had been struggling to come to terms with the death of his father some three months previously. I'm still asking myself, "Why didn't he ask me for help?" Maybe he didn't think I could. Maybe he didn't want to burden me. I'll never know. What I know is that I would have helped in any way I possibly could.

Steve was no different to you or me. How many things that are rightfully ours, or would be freely and graciously given, do we not ask for? And why? Because we imagine we'll upset people, they may think us rude, they may disagree with us, we may upset them.

What are YOU denying yourself, or those you care about? All because of what you're imagining.

What's certain is that people aren't telepathic, and if you don't ask, you'll NEVER get. If something is rightfully yours, all you need to do is ask . . . and if you don't get it, ask again, and again, and again, and again . . . It works for our children so why wouldn't it work for us?

By Steve Marriott, Managing Director, Steve Marriott Personal Coaching www.steve-marriott.co.uk

CHAPTER 2
Getting Ready for the Ask

A Handy Preparation Checklist

Question: What's the first thing you do when you plan a journey? Unless you're über-deep and asked, "For what purpose am I undertaking this journey?" you probably answered something like, "Deciding where it is I want to go." That would be my answer, too. Another word for a destination is an outcome. Knowing your outcomes in life is incredibly important and often overlooked. It's the same when you're asking for something.

Using the following points as a checklist before making a significant request will have you well prepared for success. Try it. If you're suitably prepped, you should be able to answer most of the following questions confidently. For when you're travelling light or on the road, you can download a PDF "Ask checklist" from www.soinflow.com to keep on your mobile device, notebook or in your travel bag (go to "Free" and then "Influence").

1. What is it that you want, specifically?

Admittedly, it sounds silly: if you didn't know what it was then why would you be asking for it? What I mean is that, often, people aren't entirely clear about what they want. Many people think solely of the prize and not of the wider interaction. Both are important for succeeding and for sustaining relationships. So here are some prompts to get you clear before you ask:

- Take just a moment to focus and use each of your senses to create for yourself a vivid experience of what it is you want.
- Vividly imagine the thoughts and feelings in your body and mind that lead to a satisfying outcome.
- Ask yourself, "What would be ten times better than that?" Sadly, so many people I know play small and under-value themselves. They ask for five when 300 is on the table; they ask for next week when now is available.
- Phrase what you want in the positive and avoid stating what you *don't* want, which is a common trap. Imagine walking into a bar and telling the bartender what you don't want to drink . . . It might take you a while to get what you want and you've probably annoyed everyone else in the bar at the same time. Not good.

2. For what purpose do you want it?

Do you want it for yourself, or are you asking because someone else wants it? The former is powerful; the latter less so. One of the most powerful ingredients in asking is passion, which often comes from a strong sense of mission or "purpose." When people sense genuine passion in an asker, they are often moved to action even when the "facts" are less than compelling. (Haven't we all, at some time, been really motivated by someone to do something that, in hindsight, seemed reckless, daring, silly or temporarily out of character?)

To get an idea of purpose, just ask yourself, "For what purpose do I want this?" followed by, "For what purpose do I want that?" Keep asking yourself the second question, so that you drill deeper into each response; very soon, you'll start to get a sense of your personal purpose behind the Ask (or a sense that there isn't one!).

3. How do I want it?

Getting people to agree to do something doesn't mean you have agreement on how it should be done. For example, imagine you're asking an industry expert to help you to answer some questions for a possible investor. You've managed to get them to agree to do it and they're clear on the time and date. But when they turn up they have no structure, supporting materials or slideshow, all things that this particular investor expects as standard; the "what" has been agreed, but not the all-important "how."

Be sure at some point to communicate your expectations of precisely how you'd like it done: this not only increases your chances of success but also helps maintain a healthy relationship.

4. When do I want it?

Imagine you're in the mood and you ask your partner for "some romancing." They agree. Nothing happens. You frown to convey dissatisfaction. "Oh, you mean right now?" they say. OK, a silly example, I agree, but you get what I mean. Imagine a more realistic example, where you ask somebody to finish a report for you but neglect to say when you want it: you know your deadlines and timescales – don't assume they do. Pretend that someone's pouring milk in to your tea and remember to "say when."

5. What's in it for them?

If there's one thing that truly separates masters of influence from the initiated, it's the ability to frame a proposition from the other person or group's point of view. They learn to look for what's in it for the other party: what do they stand to gain or lose from not saying, "Yes!" to you? Most people spend an Ask talking about themselves – do not be one of these selfish askers.

Spend time thinking and talking from the other party's perspective: remember that people aren't so much interested in you, they're more interested in what you can do for them. Harsh? Perhaps. Although, ultimately, we choose to associate with anyone because of how they allow us to feel around them or what they can do for us. Even selfless giving ultimately fulfils some of our own deep-seated needs or values.

6. What am I prepared to give, sacrifice or negotiate to get it?

Expect a "giving" to get a "getting." Many times you'll not have to offer anything in exchange, whether that's before, at the time or further down the line. However, understand that sometimes there'll need to be some kind of trade to get what you want. In fact, in the best relationships, there's a constant give and take, an ebb and flow of favours, requests and offers. Be prepared: is it fair of you to ask for what you want, offering nothing back in return?

7. Could I survive without it?

The zenith in asking is to feel energized and excited about what you want but without feelings of neediness or compulsion to obtain it. Seriously, and I can't stress this enough, nothing turns people off more than someone who's perceived as needy, desperate or overly attached to the prize.

When an asker's level of self-interest – what they stand to gain from asking – is so overwhelmingly high, we start to wonder whether their level of consideration for us is correspondingly low. This typically diminishes trust enough for us to back away from the exchange. "Desperation stinks!"

8. What emotional/physical state will be most conducive to getting it?

Great askers lead their audience "into state" before asking by getting into that state first themselves. For example, if your request involves some risk-taking (and, let's face it, when doesn't it?), showing nervousness may harm your outcome. If you're pitching something that is exciting and inspiring, talking and gesturing in an inspiring, exciting way will help your audience to "feel what you're saying," to move your way.

Rizzolatti's original experiments pointed to this in a real-life case of "monkey see, monkey do." The research team noticed that when the monkey watched someone bringing food to his or her mouth or licking an ice cream, the monkey's brain (monitored with electrodes) seemed to be simulating neural activity as if the monkey was performing the action itself.[1]

So, if neuroscientists generally now believe that behaviour is "state" dependent, consider this: if you feel angry, your decisions will be biased by that mood; if you feel loving, your decisions will be biased in a very different direction. Common sense, really, but so few of us pay attention to what "state" we want the other party to be in at the actual moment of asking. If you're not mindful of this, you're less in control of your results.

How do you want the other party to think and feel before, during and after the Ask? Do you want them to feel curious? Energized? Anxious? Flirty? Humorous? Resilient? The quickest way to lead them into that state is to "go there yourself" first. If you do it well, they'll follow.

9. What time and environment will be most conducive to getting it?

If you want someone to go on a date with you, you may not want to ask them when they're feeling jilted and jaded, having just acrimoniously ended a five-year relationship. If you want to ask your best friend to join you in meditation class, asking them while at a rave may not overly help your cause. Considering the timing and setting of your request is a good habit to get into.

What's more, the area of our brain that we rely on most for conscious processing is the pre-frontal cortex (PFC). The PFC uses a lot of precious glucose and so we've evolved to process as many decisions as possible non-consciously to conserve time and energy – we call these non-conscious decisions "heuristics" or "rules of thumb." We all know that when we're tired, we can't learn, think or respond as well as we usually can, so we should make sure we've thought about this beforehand, if possible.

For example, asking someone to make a complex decision in a noisy café, where their attention is limited, is risky. Asking someone to switch to your company before lunch or the end of the day, when their brain glucose level is low is not advisable (yes, a scientific reason why most salespeople line up their decision-making calls for early in the morning).[2]

As you'll read further on, even the choice of room, objects and chair they sit in will noticeably influence your audience's response.

Choose Your Ask

As you'll read in the coming pages, some Asks are more suited to certain people, situations and media than others. You'll get a sense of this quite early on. Some are more suited to larger, formal requests; others are more suited to asking a friend for a favour. Some only work in person; others will work beautifully in written formats. So, before asking, consider which Asks are most suitable for:

- The *relationship*: how well do you know your audience? How many people?
- The *request*: is it risky? Something others are doing? Collaborative? Values-based?
- The surrounding *environment*: where will you be? What will be going on around you?
- The *medium*: will it be face-to-face? An email? A written document?

Rest assured that there are many different Asks with different philosophies behind them that will work equally well in a variety of situations and audiences. After a bit of practice, you'll find yourself mentally preparing in moments or even without conscious thought, drawing on a bank of firm favourites that you enjoy.

Practical Advice before the Ask

1. Speak to the organ grinder

One of the most thoroughly condescending maxims I know and love is, "Speak to the organ grinder, not the monkey." In other words, once you're clear on what it is you want, always ask someone who can give you what it is you're asking for. If it sounds patronizing, you'd be shocked at the number of people who ask someone unable to authorize the request and then give up when they get the "No."

Recently, for example, my bank accidentally cancelled all of my bank cards, disabling us from drawing money from ATMs or buying anything, such as food. Though it was their fault, the representative I was speaking to insisted that new cards would take up to seven *working* days to arrive. Since it was a Saturday morning, that meant 12 days without cards and we had no cash in the house. The representative suggested we borrow cash from friends and family for the week or drive into the city to withdraw a large amount. I was unhappy with the advice so asked to speak to his manager. His manager had us the cards delivered by courier within three working days. The representative didn't know that this was possible.

Ask, "Can this person authorize my request?" If not, find out who can and position yourself to work with them, while being respectful to your current contact.

2. Responsive relationships matter

Who are you more likely to say, "Yes" to: someone you know intimately and trust, with a track record of delivering or someone you've just met? Are you more likely to "move along" without question when asked by a police officer or a five-year-old child? The answers are obvious, which means that, in most cases, creating phenomena like rapport, credibility, authority and trust before asking is crucial. These are some of the conditions of responsiveness. Once you've mastered the techniques in this book, you may like to find ways to create new techniques based on these conditions. They're the keys to the vault – explore ethically and responsibly!

Whether this means building a strong relationship over time before asking, instigating responsiveness conditions or capitalizing on them when they occur is up to you. My own advice would be that focusing on building strong, open, balanced relationships is key to thriving in our modern world.

3. "Yes!" is mostly emotion and gut instinct

A growing body of work on decision making from the fields of neuroscience and psychology points to the conclusion that rational thinking and facts play a far smaller part in our decisions than our egos would like to think!

Director of the famed Max Planck Institute, Gerd Gigerenzer, focuses much of his work on "gut instincts" in decision making. He concludes that our evolutionary instincts are hardwired to save time and energy in decision making by going with our inbuilt "rules of thumb." We tend to focus on "the one thing" that sways us most in a situation and this happens very early on in a given situation, as a survival mechanism. Our rules of thumb or "heuristics" take over and bias us towards comfort, power, familiarity, safety and certainty, amongst other needs. What this implies for our influencing attempts is the need to recreate these feelings in our Ask.

4. If at first you don't succeed . . .

A while back, the Results Corporation plc conducted a study in business sales which showed that 60% of sales happen after the fifth "No."

Getting to a "Yes" after that many "Not yets" requires being agile, creative and determined in looking for a different way to the prize (and not necessarily in the same phone call or meeting by the way!). The twist in their data is that 44% of business professionals give up after the first "No," 22% after the second and 14% after the third.

If, right now, you make a promise to yourself to always continue past three "No's," you're effectively putting yourself straight into the top 20% of the world's influencers – you've become that one in five statistic! And continuing past each successive "No" makes you become exponentially more rare and more effective.

Asking again isn't like Mrs Doyle from the Irish TV series *Father Ted*: it's not about saying, "Go on. Go on. Ah, go on. Go on, go on, go on, go on, go on . . ." until the other party submits. It's about purpose, asking questions, clarifying, comforting, reframing, challenging and persisting. These are skills and qualities that mainly come from an internal compass set to wanting the best for yourself and the best for the other party. Keep at it and set "the little Yes bird" free!

Are You Ready?

"With great power . . ."

Hopefully, having read through these first pages, you're now thinking more clearly about your current attitudes to asking, as well as your current abilities and opportunities. You'll have noted that our natural child-like state is to ask without inhibition; that social inhibition develops as we move into adulthood. You'll also have considered that there may be no such thing as a natural persuader: that while we do possess genetic propensities towards certain traits and abilities, they won't be realized fully without the right environment and instruction.

In Chapter 1 you've looked at some of the common inhibitors – deserving, rejection, success, discomfort and wrong peer group – and learned that they're all constructs that you can acknowledge and then put aside while you go about setting up new habits. You also have a checklist of useful points to reflect upon if you're planning your request: in essence, what do you want (specifically), what's in it for them and how might you ask? And you've some practical considerations: right person, responsive relationships, gut instinct and the power of perseverance.

And with that you're now ready to start learning the techniques that might just make a palpable difference to your results, status, experience and rewards. But remember, with great power comes great responsibility! All of the approaches featured in this book are powerful by themselves, let alone when combined. Please enjoy them responsibly, not only for your success but also for the greater good.

See you at the top. If you get there before I do, mine's a glass of red wine.

Inside every "No" egg, if you hit the shell hard enough and enough times and use the right spoon, there is a little "Yes" bird waiting to come out.

For example, when we started innocent, one of the hardest things was searching for an investor. We had no experience, no product and no name. But the one thing we had was a robust business plan. Without cash, though, we couldn't start our business at any significant scale. We tried all the VC companies in London and they all said no. We heard, "You're too young. You're all friends. You've never run a business before. You've no experience of the sector and you'll be competing against the world's biggest food and drinks companies. It is a dreadful investment opportunity."

When we were at our most disheartened, we tried a more random approach and sent out a cheeky email that simply said "does anyone know anyone rich?" in the subject line. We posted that email to every address we had (and lots we didn't). We got two responses. One of them introduced us to a man called Maurice Pinto. We sent him our business plan – and he liked us. And, unlikely as it was, just on the point of giving up, we tried a different route and we got the money.

By Richard Reed, co-founder of innocent drinks
www.innocentdrinks.co.uk

Part One

Asking with Frames in Mind

What's Frames Got to Do With It?

Underneath the surface of any communication lies a deeper structure of information that's presupposed, believed or expected to be true. We call them "frames of reference," or "frames" for short.

For example, if I ask you, "Would you like tea or coffee?" I'm assuming (a) that you're definitely having one of them, (b) that you're *not* having both drinks (or neither), (c) that other beverages, say, orange juice or water, are not on offer, even though I may have them, (d) that you would like to have your choice with hot water and drink it, rather than sing a sea shanty to the beans or leaves, (e) that you understand that I will make you the drink and bring it to you after receiving your preference.

The list could go on into a navel-gazing level of detail. The point is that in any given communication, the sender has a frame of reference and the receiver has a frame of reference. Sometimes the frames match, often they are different (ever found yourself saying, "No! That's not what I meant at all!" to someone?).

Great persuaders, with practice, are able to shape the frame that the receiver uses, to give meaning to what is happening and what is about to happen.

As mentioned earlier, our brains have cleverly evolved short cuts for processing most information, to save our conscious brains for special tasks, meaning we non-consciously absorb the "invisible" information and use it as our frame of reference in the moment. A great example of this is Harvard's research from 2000.[1]

Older individuals were subliminally exposed to either positive or negative ageing stereotypes. Then all participants faced mathematical and verbal challenges. Those exposed to the negative ageing stereotypes demonstrated a heightened heart response to stress, blood pressure and heart rate with lower test scores, compared with those exposed to positive ageing stereotypes. They weren't aware of it, but certain information was "framing" the way they perceived the task and how they performed.

To use a simile, setting a frame is like shining a spotlight on a stage. By definition, when you shine it on one area of the stage, you make the rest of the stage go dark. Setting frames guides your audience's attention in a particular way, determining what's in scope and what's out of scope.

So, frames subliminally direct our attention, prime our experience and influence how we respond next. Some frames owe their influence to contrast; some to sequence and timing; some to guiding attention to include or exclude certain ideas.

Through a variety of approaches, strong persuaders are masters of setting frames that presuppose the other party will move their way.

CHAPTER 3
Consistency

One of the most instinctual drives I observe in others and myself is the drive to justify our choices, thoughts and actions. Even when there's no one else around, the wee Gremlin in the back of our mind urges us to justify what we did and why we did it.

Often this happens beyond conscious awareness. We do it to maintain a "positive, consistent self-perception." In other words, if we consistently doubted ourselves, our motives and our behaviour, we'd lack self-esteem and confidence, thus lowering our chances of surviving and attracting a mate.

Inconsistency, or "flakiness," is generally seen in any society as a flaw. For example, reneging on a deal or saying one thing and doing another. In influence, this concept of consistency with our thoughts, choices and behaviour can be used to increase commitment to action.

In social psychology research, real-life examples of this abound, from increasing voter turnout and involvement in election campaigns to generating more appointments for door-to-door charity canvassers. The power of starting a chain of consistency is so strong that it was also used systematically to brainwash American POWs in the Korean War and in just about every cult over the last few thousand years. Taking baby steps in the direction of a particular cause (for example, signing a petition against fox hunting) even has the creeping potential to shape our self-perception in the long term.

What follows next is a reliable collection of modern commitment-gaining approaches that tap into our psychological desire for consistency.

"Not too bad . . ." is a response that seems almost prepro-grammed when asking many people, "How are you?" Although it's part of the daily ritual of life, my view is that you can leverage it by saying, "Not too bad? That seems that your default position is a level of bad?"

Now, it's not an easy challenge and you have to be very careful not to sound like a positive-thinking cliché, I grant you. I believe that with humour and open body language, you can do it in such a way that people get the point you're making (after initially thinking you're a bit odd). My point is that the value of any interaction is in its honesty and positive outlook. After all, negativ-ity is just as contagious as positivity – it's just that it's corrosive.

Try it. See how many people you can influence into being a bit more honest about how they are. In turn, I'd argue you get a more fruitful and frank discussion much earlier in the interaction, whether it's social, in turn building deeper relationships, or busi-ness, getting closer to the win-win Nirvana.

By Paul Blair, Global Organizational Development Director, Wood Group www.woodgroup.com

1. The Consistency Two-Step

Picture the scene: an American college campus, a bar. Our bartender identifies a set of regular customers; he asks half, "Will you sign a petition against drunk driving?" He makes no such request of the other half. Over the following six weeks, our bartender keeps track of which of the students in the group get drunk. Once spotted, our bartender pops a second question to them: "May I call a taxi to take you home?" Only 10% of our group who were not asked to sign the petition agreed to wait for the taxi; 58% of those who signed were willing to wait. Six times the result! Tapping into consistency – asking someone to remain consistent with something they've previously said or done – may leverage compliance.[1]

Just for a moment, imagine someone with a Harley Davidson tattoo on their arm: how likely is it that they'll ever buy a Suzuki? By declaring themselves "a Harley Davidson kind of person" their drive for consistency precludes them buying something different, even though they may agonize over the decision. Ultimately, consistency will win unless they can find the holy grail of remaining consistent and having the alternative – for example, keeping the Harley and buying the Suzuki! You may laugh at the example, but in a 2005 brand tattoo survey, 18.9% of people said that of all brands, they'd most like a Harley Davidson tattoo on their person. This was backed up with data from tattoo parlours in Australia, which confirmed that the most requested brand for inking was . . . Harley Davidson.

Try it

What small action, step, thought or request would it take to get your audience wearing a "you" tattoo – in other words, to take a very small step towards you, your products and services or your cause?

In times when we break consistency, we suffer a kind of mental anguish psychologists term "cognitive dissonance," meaning our actions are out of step with our self-perception. It's horrid. Thankfully, we're quite skilled at finding ways round it, so it doesn't last for long. For example, imagine someone who's giving up smoking for health reasons at their children's request but lapses into smoking again, in a moment of weakness. They suffer the torturous "cognitive dissonance" (I told everyone I'd quit but I'm smoking again) for a day or so until realizing that they weren't hanging out with the bosses at work, with whom they used to smoke. That means their career prospects were being adversely affected as a non-smoker, which means less security for the family, less money, less healthy food and fewer holidays. Smoking now aligns with their promise and value of being there for the family, to care and provide for them. So, actually, smoking is benefitting all of them. Phew! Dissonance sidestepped. We rationalize (rational lies) our more dubious thoughts and behaviour to avoid dissonance at all costs.

◎ Try it

Ask the two-step:

1. *Pose a question* that has your audience members raise a hand (literally or figuratively), in that their answer says something about them as a person.
2. *Make a request* of them that invites them to be consistent with that self-concept.

---

2. Foot-in-the-Door

As a technique, starting with a small commitment that leads onto a bigger commitment is often referred to as the "Foot-in-the-door" technique. It's well documented and widely known in business that it's easier to get a large sale after your customer has agreed to a smaller initial purchase.[2] Jehovah's Witnesses use this technique, asking the homeowner if he or she would be open to taking a copy of their magazine. If you accept, the Jehovah's Witnesses call back a few days later for a longer conversation to see what you thought – since you were interested. Otherwise why would you have taken the magazine?

Business websites often use this in the form of a "squeeze page." You'll have seen it countless times before. It works like this: they have some interesting material for you *if* you enter your details for them (your details are of high value to them, for marketing purposes). If you submit your details to download the resources, the business has a legitimate reason to follow up with you: you've declared you're interested in the topic as well as giving them permission to use your details.

Another common example of this is the large add-on sell or cross sell. Once the customer has committed to the purchase, a smaller value add-on sell will be offered. No one, to my mind, does this better than the sales juggernaut that is Vistaprint, the business stationery supplies website. Once you've uploaded your design for, let's say, business cards and committed to the checkout process, the ingenious designers take you through a highly compelling sales process. You are presented with your beloved designs on more expensive items ranging from mugs to T-shirts, fridge magnets to calendars to add to your order (all time-sensitive offers, of course). It's worth buying some business cards from them just to replicate the process!

However, my favourite example of this is from a social psychologist named Steven J. Sherman. Imagine you live in Bloomington, Indiana, USA. One day, you receive a call from someone running a survey. They ask you whether you'd be willing to spend three hours collecting money for the American Cancer Research Society. Not wanting to seem antisocial, you say, "Yes, I'd be someone who'd do that kind of thing."

Now fast-forward to a few days later. A representative from the American Cancer Society calls, thanks you for your stance on the matter and asks you to come good on your intention by volunteering to canvass in your area . . .

In the study[3] this led to a seven-fold increase in recruitment. That's not to be sneezed at. Tapping into someone's self-perception and then asking them to remain consistent with that is one of the most powerful approaches I know.

As the father of social psychology, Robert Cialdini, points out, "the most powerful cocktail is when the commitment is active, public, effortful and volunteered by them."

 Try it

Rather than immediately asking for what you want, ask first for something that's far smaller and easy to agree with to get the commitment ball rolling, and then ask for it.

3. Invisibly Consistent

In keeping with this theme of consistency, let's look at some incredibly simple ways to trigger this "two-step," so you can line up compliance with your second request through a seemingly irrelevant first request.

In 1990, consumer researcher Daniel Howard ran a study that nearly doubled compliance, simply by demonstrating good manners. When called by telephone and asked whether the Hunger Relief Committee charity could visit them to sell cookies for the good cause, only 18% of the public accepted. In the second experiment, members of the public were asked, "How are you feeling this evening?" to which most people replied, "fine" or "good." It'd be taboo to answer, "Actually, I'm a bit upset with my kids and the house is a right mess . . ." to a total stranger – it's just too intimate for the quality of relationship at hand. Having admitted all was well, 32% of people in the second experiment agreed to a visit (and 89% of those people bought cookies).

Another simple trigger I've found useful is, "Can you help me please?" Not only would it be rude and taboo to say, "No" but also agreeing to this makes it more likely your audience will agree to your next request. After all, they did say they would help you, didn't they?

Again, when sitting on trains with laptops, iPads, bags and various items, what do you do when you need to go to powder your nose? Do you take a risk and leave your stuff on your seat? Do you pack it away and unpack it upon your return? I often notice travellers looking slightly nervous or uncomfortable at this juncture, especially if they notice me noticing that (obviously, I'm eyeing up their stuff). The simple solution is to ask, "Would you be kind enough to look after my stuff for me, please?" Who would reply, "No, I'm simply not kind enough to do so?" Moriarty's research in 1975 showed that people would be nearly five times more likely to pursue a thief who snatched someone's stuff if they'd been asked to look after it by the owner.[4] "Would you keep my place in this queue please? I forgot to get one thing," is another useful everyday request to kick-start consistency. Try it!

Try it

Get into the habit of asking small consistency requests, such as, "How are you feeling?" "How's business?" "Would you keep an eye on this for me please?" "Would you keep my place, please?"

---

4. Make Them Work for It

We saw earlier that commitment is enhanced when it is "effortful." Why is this?

A recent study on "hazing," the term used to describe harsh initiation ceremonies and rituals, included over 60,000 student athletes from 2400 colleges and universities. In her report, Dr Nadine C. Hoover of Alfred University writes,

> "One in five was subjected to unacceptable and potentially illegal hazing. They were kidnapped, beaten or tied up and abandoned. They were also forced to commit crimes.
> Two-thirds were yelled or sworn at, forced to wear embarrassing clothing or forced to deprive themselves of sleep, food or personal hygiene."[5]

This bizarre way of gaining access into a tribe has happened since the dawn of man across cultures. Death during initiations is not uncommon. Many cults have similar rituals for initiation and access. Many religions have positive versions of these rituals, which signal a break with the old life and an acceptance of a new life.

From a psychological viewpoint, these rituals are there to increase commitment to the cause, the group or the ideology. The harder we work for something we want to obtain, the more we are prepared to suffer in its attainment and the more we value it, promote it and protect it. So, without hazing people, how can we use this principle of "effort = commitment" in our persuasion plays?

The simple answer is that the more you invite your audience to say or do during the interaction, the more committed they become. Instead of filling out forms and asking them personal details, such as bank account details and earnings, think about letting them fill out the form. As well as being more respectful, the act of filling out the form will create more commitment to your cause.

One great example I've experienced is something I term "Apply to Buy." It usually happens at the pre-appointment phase and essentially involves your audience filling out a form to qualify for an appointment with you. It can include a section for cost projections (their current costs and a comparison to show projected savings), a section for bank details (to get over the "pain" of supplying them later on) and a section asking why they are interested in, need or would benefit from your service. As well as this being useful information for you, it kick starts the process of consistency in them.

> **Try it**
>
> Get your audience to work for it. Have them offer the benefits. Ask them to fill out an "Apply to Buy" form before an appointment.

5. Paltry Requests

In 2011, I ran a little experiment of my own on LinkedIn. I wanted to run a version of the paper "Increasing compliance by legitimizing paltry contributions: when even a penny helps."[6]

In the experiment, researchers went door to door, posing as fundraisers for the American Cancer Research Society. Half of the residents ("test subjects") were asked, "Would you be willing to help by giving a donation?" The other half were asked the same, followed by, "Even a penny will help!"

They found the likelihood of contribution doubled with the second statement, with no difference in average contribution size. My interpretation was this: asking people if they'd help with a *pro-social* act triggered a desire to be consistent with a positive self-image. Then, immediately lowering the barrier to follow through made it far more likely they'd get involved. I wanted to see if it worked, so I sent out two sets of recommendation requests:

Version one:

Dear . . . ,

Hi there – hope you're well and thriving!

Would you be an angel and help me reach my goal to get over 100 recommendations by the end of April? There's a psychological experiment built into this – I'll share the results in May!

My continuing thanks in advance for helping me out. It's appreciated.

Haider

Version two:

Dear . . . ,

Hi there – hope you're well and thriving!

Would you be an angel and help me reach my goal to get over 100 recommendations by the end of April?

I'm after a one-word recommendation from you! (e.g. Inspirational! Transparent! Wacky!) That's it! If, when you start writing, you feel creative, feel free to add more, but even one word will be appreciated, when you've 60 seconds.

There's a psychological experiment built into this – I'll share the results in May!

My continuing thanks in advance for helping me out. It's appreciated.

Haider

The results were consistent with the experiment from the groovy '70s, with two particularly interesting angles. Just over twice as many people responded to the "even one word" version – 44 (version two) versus 21 (version one). Of the 44 who responded to the "even one word" request, only 14 actually used one word to describe me: 30 used an average of 33.45 words, 33 times what was suggested, and similar to the 31.1 words used by those who responded to version one.

The bottom line is that asking for a trivial effort produced a greater response rate, equal quality (arguably, greater) and similar word quantity. Making the "barrier to action" low enough that it's seen as a "no brainer" is a useful technique where a social norm for contribution exists. I suggest that when you're looking next to get commitment from volunteers, direct reports, peers, bosses or clients, you might use a version of this after you make a request. For example:

- "Could we meet next week? Even meeting for two or three minutes would help."
- "Would you like to invest? Even a down payment of a penny would secure it."
- "Are you willing to support me? Even just allowing me to say to others you support it would work."
- "Are you up for signing off this project? Even just authorizing a small pilot would be valuable."

The journey of a thousand miles begins with a single step. Remember the unassuming and long-term impact of paltry requests. Consider using it this week, even using it only once on email will help.

◉ Try it

Try asking for something that is ridiculously small compared to what your audience would expect to give in such a situation.

Consistency: A Summary

In this chapter you may have noted that:

- We have a deeply primal drive to justify our choices, thoughts and actions in a way that can be seen as consistent and in keeping with our self-perception or public image.
- The consistency two-step involves asking your audience to offer information, make a promise or hold their hand up to identify with a cause, idea or way of being to which your subsequent request holds them accountable.
- After behaving in a way that is not consistent with our private or public image, we rationalize (that is, tell ourselves "rational lies") our behaviour away to avoid cognitive dissonance.

- Once we agree to a small request, we're far more likely to agree to a bigger request compared to if we'd been asked for the bigger request in the first place.
- Even a simple comment, such as, "How are you doing this evening?" or "How's business?" can commit people so that they respond more favourably to you afterwards.
- We attach greater value and emotional importance to things which are harder for us to obtain or are more effortful.
- When a request is seen as paltry, we're likely to give more than asked for.

Now that you have these insights, how might you use some of these approaches to:

- Commit a customer to placing an order?
- Convince an employee to behave in a different way?
- Have someone increase their support for your organization?

In the next chapter you'll learn some pioneering, high-yield techniques for changing the conversation entirely from, "Do I?" to "Which one will I?"

CHAPTER 4
Same and Different

"If it's familiar, it hasn't eaten you yet," is a quote I love from Drake Bennett of *Bloomberg Businessweek*. While we're sharing, one of my favourite Hollywood stories is when Dan O'Bannon and Ronald Shusett, writers of the film *Alien*, pitched it to Hollywood studios simply as "*Jaws* in Space."

We're programmed to like what's familiar to us purely because it's not a risk to us. Back in the 1960s, Robert Zajonc's experiments uncovered what we now call the *Mere Exposure Effect* – meaning that the number of times we are exposed to certain stimuli positively influences our preferences for those stimuli. Other landmark studies have shown that when people are faced with a choice between two gambles, they will pick the more familiar one. Sometimes, they even pick the more familiar gamble when the odds of winning are lower.[1] So, it seems the writers of *Alien* understood processing fluency at a deep level. Presenting a film that radically departed in content and style from what the public was used to still needed a touch of familiarity to clinch the deal. It didn't hurt that their point of reference was a blockbuster classic.

Familiarity enables easy mental processing, saves energy and so feels fluent. So, in our minds, we tend to equate the feeling of fluency with familiarity. Put another way, we infer familiarity when a stimulus feels easy to process. More difficult to read, pronounce and/or understand means more foreign, less known, more risky.

A raft of different studies over the years shows how the ease of processing ideas, names or words affects our decision making. For example, test subjects perceived a hypothetical food additive with a name that was harder to pronounce – *Hnegripitrom* – as being more harmful than one with an easier to pronounce name – *Magnalrox-ate*.[2] Deep analysis indicates that listed companies with stock ticker codes that are easier to pronounce (such as AAPL, GOOG) trade more profitably in the long term.[3] We even "smile" in our brains when we see objects that look easy to pick up, compared to complex objects.[4]

1. A Familiar Contrast

If simple, fluent familiarity attracts us and complex, disfluent unfamiliarity repels us, we can leverage this in a myriad of ways. If your industry offers a high number of complicated solutions, the logical approach is to radically simplify your product and offering.

Telecoms companies have done this in the last couple of years with success – Three Mobile's *The One Plan* and T-Mobile's *The Full Monty* remove the "Which tariff?" conversation from the mix entirely. When Steve Jobs returned to Apple in 1997, he radically cut the product line, not only to focus business efforts, drive improvements and manage costs but also to simplify the choices for customers. It was part of what turned the company around from bankruptcy to the world's most valuable company two decades later.

If your industry doesn't have a backdrop of complexity, the most straightforward way I know is to create one. Simply present one or two options that create a degree of disfluency, followed by the option you prefer, presented in an easy, familiar, fluent format.

For example, which of the following options would you lean towards if you were a teenager: "You can go for party option one, which will be frivolity *ad absurdum* for a loquacious congregation like yours, or you can go for party option two, which will be seriously fun for you and your crazy mates – up to you?"

I suppose the only caveat to be aware of is where complexity is expected and valued, for example, if you are evaluating something with a high-tech edge to it such as processors in computers, chemicals or minerals in household equipment. However, just like *Alien*, it's worth adding in simple terms what benefits that brings, too.

Try it

Create options. Make the first options disfluent and slightly more complicated; use words with a greater number of syllables or use a touch of industry jargon. Follow this with a simple, straightforward option, articulated in a plain, easy to understand way.

---

2. Undesired to Desired

Another great way to intentionally create a perception of extra fluency that I have used many times is to present an undesired option followed by the desired option. Although it may seem odd to do this at the point of making your request, it works.

After taking the time to understand what your audience wants and doesn't want, it's simply a case of first recapping what they don't want, layering in a little complexity to create a sense of disfluency before presenting a simple, attractive version of what they do want. It has the added bonus of showing your audience that you've been listening, you're confirming their thoughts with them and keeping them in the conversation. Very respectful.

A visual way to do this is to show the undesired option in black and white or out of focus in some way next to the desired option in fully focused, clear vibrant colour. This heightens appreciation of the colour image more than if it had just been viewed in isolation. I'm not saying I've ever done this subtly featuring slightly defocused competitor logos next to my own sharp company logo, but you get the idea! It's an idea that's often used in television or magazine adverts, to show the transition from rainy, drab and dreary "before" to sunny, vibrant and cheery "after." In fact, the next time you see "before and after" cosmetic shots, check to see which photograph appears to have been lit more professionally and livened up – it's always the "after" shot.

Try it

First, frame the least preferred option in a slightly complex, disfluent way to provide a positive contrast for your preferred, simple, fluent option. Render the undesired option as a lower quality, less coloured or defocused image and your preferred option in full colour, bright and high quality.

3. Rejection then Retreat (Door-in-the-Face Technique)

A leader at an Irish client of ours wrote me a letter of thanks after attending a workshop I ran that included this Ask.

In her email, she explained how she returned home after the workshop and asked her boyfriend if they could start making plans to buy a new kitchen and redecorate the living room. After she picked him back up from the floor, her beleaguered beau replied that even though they were doing well, doing two rooms together would break the bank. She sighed, looked slightly disappointed and then suggested they "Just start with the kitchen this year," to which he eagerly agreed. "In truth," she revealed to me, "I only wanted the kitchen done. The living room is fine for now." She knew that if she'd asked only for the kitchen, the response would have been less favourable, less enthusiastic and with less commitment on her boyfriend's part.

Professional negotiators we work with know to always build a buffer into their figures: ask for more than you expect to get, give away less than you're able to and expect the others at the table to have built in a buffer as well. Usually, our clients who ask big and give small come away with better results.

Before we even get to the research around this, we intuitively know that when we haggle, are rejected but ultimately arrive at a better deal than the one we started at, we feel satisfied. If we'd named our terms and got them immediately, there'd always be a nagging doubt in the back of our mind that it was too easy; perhaps we could have asked for more? However, bartering for a deal leaves us with a sense that we got the best deal possible. So, not only does asking big bring you rewards, it helps your audience feel better about the result they have secured. A "win–win."

In a fabulous experiment over 30 years ago, a group of researchers approached students on campus, posing as the "County Youth Counselling Programme."[5] In the first version of the experiment, researchers asked the students whether they'd be willing to volunteer to look after a group of troubled youths on a day trip to the zoo, unpaid: 17% accepted; 83% refused. In the second version, the only difference was that a significantly larger request was made before the zoo request – spending two hours per week for at least two years in the role of counsellor to the troubled youths. The result? Three times as many students accepted the zoo gig. Why?

There are two reasons why this approach works so powerfully. The first is that we are hardwired for rapport and social bonding – we hate to reject (or say "No" to) each other. As explained in Chapter 1, the work of Zhou, Zheng, Zhou and Guo indicates that the old cliché, "This is going to hurt me as much as it hurts you," isn't far wrong, at least emotionally. When we reject someone, we instinctively feel more inclined to help him or her or agree to his or her next request. In other words, it triggers "reciprocity" and the desire for an oxytocin rush.

The second ingredient is "perceptual contrast." Perceptual contrast is an interesting and well-documented phenomenon in psychology.

If you'd like to try it yourself, you can take three bowls: fill bowl one with very hot water, bowl two with room temperature water and bowl three with very icy water. Put a hand in bowl one and the other in bowl three for a short time. Then put both hands in bowl two and notice how the "hot hand" now feels cold and the "cold hand" now feels hot! The contrast, or differential, is what we respond to, not the actual factual data. It's counterintuitive because we see ourselves as rational creatures when, in fact, we are anything but.

The only caveat here is that if we are reckless and make our Ask too extreme, we risk damaging not only our results but also our relationships. The trick is to ask just high enough to provoke an initial "No!" response before looking slightly disappointed and repackaging a more palatable offer. My advice to influencers is generally that the extreme request should be within the bounds of reality: that there should be some comparison, benchmark or precedent as a backdrop to your Ask.

◉ Try it

Get clear on what you actually want and then create an initial request that is just extreme enough to produce a "No!" response (70% more investment than you need, three weeks quicker delivery time when you only want three days quicker, a new kitchen, living room and furniture when you just want a new kitchen). Then, looking or sounding slightly deflated, ask for what you really want as a concession. You could phrase this as, "Oh, all right then (sigh). In that case, how about . . ."

---

4. That's Not All . . . (TNA)

I've attended my fair share of business conferences over the years where experts do their public speaking bit from the stage followed by a one-time-only deal for the audience. If you've been to enough of them, which perhaps you have, and pay enough attention to the structure of their pitch, which perhaps you have, you'll see the core framework of the final request. If you haven't been to such conferences, watch some TV shopping channels to see the same process in action.

It struck me between the eyes at a conference some years ago, where "the man who sold the Brooklyn Bridge," Paul Hartunian, used this on a grand scale. He deftly persuaded me, my colleague and about 300 other frenzied members of the audience to spring into action and secure his amazing offer at the back of the conference room, before the limited amount of deals ran out. There was nearly a stampede. I clearly remember feeling wild sensations of blossoming opportunity mixed with swelling anxiety as I battled the mob to sign up.

How does it work? The speaker presents what we think is the deal, extolling its virtues and benefits with passion in their delivery and asks us to take action. However, without giving us much time to think, they roll out the "That's not all" technique.[6]

They typically say, "But that's not all! For the first n people, for the next five minutes only, this is what you'll also get . . ." What follows is a list of deal sweeteners, each followed by "a value of '£n'," resulting in a total usual package price of '£N,' (including the main product). However, if we act now, the entire package will only cost us less than the main component by itself.

Critically, this is a very different kind of psychological phenomenon to the making of an unsuccessful request then offering a discount. Burger's research concluded that it's the *immediacy* of the added value that creates the effect by removing your audience's time to critique the first offer. Like "Rejection then Retreat," the TNA technique has two effects on us. First, it makes us feel that we are receiving concessions from the presenter, initiating reciprocity (see Chapter 8). Second, it provides a contrast for the next part of the deal to look even better.

In one experiment, Burger increased sales of cupcakes and cookies from 40% (a cupcake and two cookies for ¢75) to 73% (a cupcake for

¢75 and two cookies "for free"). In another, he increased sales from 44% (one cupcake for ¢75) to 73% (one cupcake for $1, but immediately discounted to ¢75).

 Try it

Plan out your TNA. Immediately after presenting your regular offer and without waiting for a response, offer a sweetener to have your audience say, "Yes!"

---

5. Freedom Shopping

This is a highly controversial exercise that I sometimes use for people who need more confidence, are terrible with rejection and would like to raise their asking game. Although people are initially uncomfortable with it, the epiphany they sometimes have is astonishing.

I developed it from life coach Jamie Smart's version of an approach by psychologist Paul Watzlawick. In his book *Change: Principles of Problem Formation and Problem Resolution* (1974), Watzlawick is dealing with a young man who is unable to finish his thesis, due to anxiety. Without sharing his reasoning, Watzlawick instructs the student to go into three shops and make absurd requests. The student does so, experiences a subtle change in his sense of self and completes his thesis shortly thereafter. Jamie Smart's build on this was to go into a shop and ask for something you know they can't offer, for example, asking for a pizza in a fast-food hamburger shop.

"Freedom shopping," my extension to this, also involves intentionally courting rejection to realize that, while uncomfortable in the moment, life goes on and you get over it.

It also draws on mindfulness, perceptual contrast and reciprocity, making it a rocket-powered request.

My workshop students enter a high street shop and ask for something they are confident will result in rejection: a dress in an electrical shop, a sandwich in a sports clothing shop or a sofa in a sandwich shop, perhaps. Once they receive the rejection, they ask for something smaller and give a reason (see "Just because . . ." in Chapter 13). It often sounds like this, "Oh. Well, might I have something for free *because* I'm on a confidence-building course and am supposed to return with a little something."

The aim of the exercise is not to see what you can get, or even to "get" something. The aim is to build your rejection muscle and practise making bigger, bolder, more outlandish requests. *However*, students often come back with free gifts – on average 50% of the time. Over the years, these gifts have ranged in value from bags of gourmet coffee to headphones, from kids' toys to toiletries (in fact, one sandwich chain is so consistently generous, I won't spend money with any other café, if possible!). One group I worked with in London got so carried away, they returned to the workshop 20 minutes late with bagsful of gifts, totalling about 40 pounds each, wearing a feeding-frenzied expression on their faces. Inappropriate, perhaps, but the next time they're pitching for venture capital, they'll almost certainly aim higher and get more and leave their audience feeling satisfied that they struck a great bargain.

Try it

Walk into a shop and ask for something outlandish, with a smile on your face, expecting a rejection. Next, ask for something comparatively smaller for free, giving a reason why. Whatever the outcome, keep smiling, thank them and leave graciously.

6. Choices: Gold, Silver, Bronze

Now that you know about perceptual contrast, you'll appreciate why, "Was £1,499 . . . now £799" is so attractive to us as consumers. Great persuaders know this intimately. As soon as one amount (which could be time, price, share, commitment, etc.) is presented, mentioned or even "accidentally" shown, it becomes fixed in the audience's mind as an "anchor" to which thinking and decisions inevitably become "biased" – almost as if the anchor is strangely magnetic, which it is. At this juncture, presenting a second, contrasting amount, which is closer to the original expectation is received with exponentially more enthusiasm than if the second amount had been presented on its own.

So, following the theory of ABCs (anchors, bias and contrast), a super high price, followed by a more reasonable price will be more attractive than just presenting the reasonable price on its own. Asking for someone to complete a task now, then conceding that they can complete it by the end of today instead, is more attractive than just asking them to complete it by the end of today.

Behavioural economics researcher, Dan Ariely, ran a fascinating experiment based on a chance encounter with *The Economist* website.

Accidentally, subscription to the magazine was being offered in three flavours: an online only option for $59, a print only option for $125 and an online plus print option for . . . $125!

He was intrigued enough to run this experiment with his students. When three options were presented, 16% displayed a preference for the online only option and 84% preferred the combination option, print and online. When the unintentional combination was removed, 68% of people preferred the online only option and only 32% went with the print only option.

Hypothetically, from a revenue-generation perspective, the inclusion of the "mistaken" offer led to a 43% uplift.

Why? Ariely explains that our perception of value is relative not absolute. In other words, we may not have a reference for what the value of a year's subscription to *The Economist* is, but we do know that print and online for the same price as print only is a better deal. For that reason, we are (a) more likely to commit and (b) more likely to commit bigger when directed to evaluate competing options, than compared to offering a solitary option. Choices, it seems, increase compliance and extent of compliance. Our internal conversation moves away from, "Do I or don't I?" to "Which one would I?"

In business parlance, we have shifted from a selling conversation to a negotiating conversation: the "sale" has already been made.

One of the ways my company uses this in business is to give clients options in our proposals, commonly referred to as "Gold, Silver and Bronze." It's a great approach to use for managing the expectations of people who expect you to "do more with less," at work or in your social life.

Using the approaches I've just outlined, we offer three options. Three seems to be the optimal number of choices, by the way, supported by some cute research[7] – cutting the number of product choices consistently increases revenue. Sheena Iyengar, author of *The Art of Choosing* says,

> "I don't think people don't want a lot of choice. People will say they want a lot of choice but I don't think that's what they really want. What they really want is a better choosing experience. They want to feel competent during the choosing process and they want to feel confident that what they have chosen is a 'good' choice."

So, the Gold option comes first; this is the option that delivers on what they need, gives them what they want and also adds in some more value-added work. It's attractive and advisable but more than they'd budgeted for and perhaps not essential right now. It usually produces a "sharp-intake-of-breath" moment.

Next, when they come to the Silver option, they see a scope and price tag that is as they expected; they experience a sense of relief and reinforcement – all is right with the world.

Finally, they cast their eye over the Bronze option. It's the budget option and leaves out some of the more essential elements they need but it's marginally cheaper. In comparison to Silver, it hardly seems worth doing.

Everything points towards Silver and in all my years on consulting, managing and selling, I've never had anyone go for Bronze or Gold.

Of course, sometimes they've gone for, "No, thanks," as the sales process progresses but it's important to understand that the only option they ever consider, regardless of whether they follow through, is Silver.

For struggling managers, it's a great one to use when asked to do the impossible. Classifying the option you want as Silver and outlining what resources you'll need to make the various options happen (time, money, training, extra employees and so on) helps manage expectations very clearly indeed.

 Try it

Get clear about what you want; call this the Silver option. Create an option that is comparatively lavish and a lot more of an investment of time, money and/or commitment, for example; call this Gold. Create an option that is slightly less than what's wanted or needed but the upside is that it's less of an investment than Silver, marginally; call that Bronze. Now present your choices in the following order: Gold, Silver, Bronze.

7. Ugly Twin

Another piece of Ariely research that is useful for visually influencing people's choice is his "ugly twin" research. He showed groups of people a headshot of a male avatar named Tom and one named Jerry and asked them to say which avatar was more physically attractive. Straightforward, perhaps? The twist, however, was that Ariely added a third avatar to the line up – "ugly twin Jerry" for some, "ugly twin Tom" for others.

Now, rationally, we'd expect whoever is more attractive, Tom or Jerry, to receive the nod, wouldn't we? The results showed something different. The avatar that had its ugly twin next to it was consistently voted "most attractive." In other words, when "ugly twin Jerry" was around, Jerry was most attractive. When "ugly twin Tom" was around, Tom was most attractive.[8]

Our perception of value is based on relatives (excuse the pun), not absolutes.

Again, could this partly explain why "before and after" shots are so prevalent in cosmetics advertising?

Try it

If you're visually displaying images, choices or products, consider featuring three together. Two of these should look very similar to each other: put the very similar looking older, lower quality or less attractive option right beside the pretty one.

---

8. Time for a Rhyme?

Rhymes are a great example of where fluency is used in advertising campaigns, especially jingles, because research has shown that rhyming increases influence. See if you can complete these famous slogans: "(What?) Means Heinz," "A Mars a day helps you work, rest and (what?)" and "Once you pop, you can't (what?)." All of them are instantly memorable and therefore perceived as credible. Even half-rhymes such as, "Nothing goes together like a pint and Castella," or "You can't fit quicker than a Kwik Fit fitter," worm their way into our minds as credible statements, purely because they're simple and sound familiar. There's no comeback to such a rhyming statement, just as, "He who smelled it, dealt it," meant conceding shame and defeat in my earlier years.

◉ Try it

Playfully, sing or include a rhyming statement in your final request, for example, "Those who've been through it, wanna do it. Do you want to do it?" Or, reaching out to shake hands (see "The outstretched hand" in Chapter 7!) try, "Goodbye debts, no regrets . . . What do you say?" or "I can't wait to get started on this! Let's shake it in and rake it in!"

---

9. The Font of Success

In tests, fonts that are easier to read make us twice as likely to opt for a product[9] although research exists that shows that unusual fonts help us remember the information more.[10] What really fascinates me is that in the tests, where subjects have to read instructions in disfluent fonts or illegible handwriting, they report the task itself as more difficult, not the instructions. This is a crucial distinction: the disfluency is passed onto the task, not the instructions. It's subtle, yet impactful.

◉ Try it

- Make sure your font or handwriting is clean, clear, simple and large enough to catalyze processing fluency.
- Use spaces, images, plenty of white space, short sentences and paragraphs where possible.
- Keep your words simple: complicated writing creates disfluency and is perceived as unintelligent.[11]
- *Use elaborate, stylized or unusual fonts and handwriting if your aim is to have your message remembered!*

Same and Different: A Summary

In this chapter you may have noted that:

- Our minds tend toward options that give us a high degree of familiarity and fluency because they're safe and easy to process.
- Simplicity is king.
- Creating disfluency as a contrast to fluency heightens the perception of fluency.
- Recapping what's not wanted before what is wanted heightens desire.
- Contrasting a big demand (going for a "No!") with a subsequent reasonable demand makes the reasonable demand more likely.
- Making your offer then immediately adding a "That's not all . . ." creates reciprocity and a contrast.
- Giving three options is best: most costly first, preferred second, cheap and cheerful last.
- When we compare similar items and one is slightly less attractive, our attraction to the pretty one is heightened irrationally.
- Messages that rhyme are more credible.
- Simple fonts persuade.

Now that you have these insights, how might you use some of these approaches to:

- Secure a big increase in salary or resource from your boss or bank manager?
- Enlist a child to do some housework?
- Have a partner choose the venue you'd like?

In the next chapter you'll learn favourite Asks from the world of business: time-honoured and good to go.

CHAPTER 5
Ready for Business

Although I've aimed to use as much science and rigour to give you even more confidence to use the successful approaches you're absorbing in this book, it's certainly not my opinion that scientific research must exist for any technique to be worthwhile. If it works, it works – simple.

Over the last 15 years in the influence business, I've learned, used and taught many techniques for which there is no official proof and they bring strong results for clients. The business domain exemplifies a "survival of the fittest ideas" market: the risk involved in getting it wrong costs jobs, money, time, livelihoods and credibility. So, when business finds something that works, you know that academic validation of it will follow years later.

It's always nice to rock a little bit of old school during a new school gig, so what follows next is a selection of business classics, *go to* approaches that will undoubtedly help you as much as they've helped me, my colleagues and my clients.

1. Requests as Opportunities

There's an old adage in sales, "People love to buy but hate to be sold to." It holds very true in today's climate, where the number of attempts

Too often when requests are made, the benefits given to validate the request are just not enough, whether it relates to emotional benefit or financial benefit. Life is simpler when all the information and facts are presented simultaneously.

In my experience, fantastic thoughts, ideas or requests that could add significant value often don't get the consideration they deserve as the benefit analysis has not been given due care and attention. When making the request, understand what the person who will ultimately grant it will need to know to make a quick decision, anticipate the questions that will run through their head at the time and do your level best to have answered them there and then. When this is not the case and more time is required to validate the suggestion, the moment can be lost.

I believe that organizations that get this right tend to be the ones that are admired for moving at pace, effecting change and empowering people to make things happen.

By Rob Papps, Managing Director UK, Nando's UK
www.nandos.co.uk

to influence us through various media increases daily: watch this, think about this, listen to this, buy this, donate to this, don't eat that – eat this, help me with this, don't do this, friend me, poke me, like my post, please have this finished by, call me.

Most people, at times, feel slightly oppressed and overwhelmed by this barrage of self-interested marketing and attention seeking and switch off as a result. The last thing we want when making a request is for our audience to switch off. We need them primed, engaged and ready to hear what they need to do next.

So, a fundamental philosophy in asking is to package your request in terms of how it can benefit or add value to your audience. Thinking of this in terms of the opportunity that it may afford them, should they accept, is a potent style of asking to build into your muscle.

For our negotiation students, we sometimes talk about "Power Analysis" in this respect. Often, as they talk about their current deals, they're of the mindset that their counterpart has all the "power" and calls all the shots. Often, a simple repositioning of the variable at play allows them to see that not only is that untrue but, in fact, they hold a powerful position and doing business on their terms is an opportunity not to be missed.

For example, if you've lots on and you need your child to help with the housework, you might say, "If you're able to help me with the (insert chores here), I'll definitely have enough time to play football with you before dinner. What do you think?" Inherent in that statement is a potential gain for them, which dwarfs any pain involved.

At work, if you need to delegate some of your workload, this could be "an opportunity for one of your team to get some valuable enrichment, experience and exposure to help their career." Compare it to, "I need your help." How does that come across?

Though you may need your investors' money, *they* have a "rare and time-limited opportunity to get in at ground level, with a company that's going to generate good exposure for them, as well as profit."

Inexperienced askers see the act of asking as "putting on people," inconveniencing them and slightly awkward; experienced askers always think, "How could accepting this benefit my audience?"

> ### Try it
>
> Whatever you want to ask, think about how agreeing with the request presents your audience with an opportunity that they will value and would not otherwise have.

2. The Sharp Angle

Before looking at the verbal articulation of the sharp angle or *conditional* request, I think it's useful to know when to bring this bad boy out. And it is a bad boy, make no mistake. Direct sellers have dined out on this one for decades.

Quite often in our interactions, our audience presents what is known in business as a *buying signal*. A buying signal is a question or statement that indicates that your audience is thinking about moving ahead in their mind. Obvious buying signals may be:

"That's a good idea!"
"Ooh . . . Brilliant!"
"How much is it?"
"How long does it take to set up?"
"Can we tweak a few bits?"
"What happens if I have a problem with it?"

All these questions show that your audience is playing the movie of accepting it in their mind's eye, based on certain criteria being met.

Other buying signals are less obvious: objections, resistance, concerns and reactance are all buying signals, unless it's a flat, "No." If someone objects, they are simply giving you a *condition that needs to be satisfied* before they can move forward. For example:

"I'm too tired."

"I can't afford it."

"I'm nervous – I'm not sure people will go for this approach."

"It's too gaudy."

"It'll take too long – I've not enough time."

It can sometimes be really helpful to use the sharp angle to ask for a show of commitment from everyone before moving ahead. In its simplest form, the sharp angle is: "If I could, would you?" For example, "If (I/we/you) could (make it less energetic/make it more affordable/ get the proof you need/make it more subtle/make it quick), would you (be happy to move forward with it)?"

Asking it requests your audience to show their hand: are you serious about this? If we can get you the condition you say you need, do we have an agreement? Many times, I've seen people spring a leak at this stage and produce a dozen reservations, objections and excuses. This shows that they're not yet ready for a final Ask and I'd suggest you go back a few steps to asking questions. If you haven't got time, why not try "What would have to happen for you to move forward with this?" to get the criteria for agreement.

It's worth emphasizing that you must be able to deliver on your conditional offer ("If I could do 'x' . . ."); otherwise you'll lose the agreement and potentially weaken your influence for next time around. At worst, you may damage the relationship, so always under-promise and over-deliver.

 Try it

When you hear a strong buying signal and you sense you are close to the moment of truth, try asking, "If we could . . . would you . . . ?"

3. Contingency Contracts

A lovely variation of the sharp angle is the contingency contract. It's particularly useful when you're attempting to reach agreement with someone who either makes a bold assertion that they or you can't substantiate or unwaveringly demands something that is costly to you.

For example, a supplier claims you'll easily sell 300 of its new line of T-shirts in your shop over the summer months. They push you to take an order for 300 – that's far larger than the order of 50 you wanted. The buy price on offer, though, is an attractive one (£2.50 per unit based on an order of 300, compared to £4 per unit based on an order of 50). It's on a "no returns" basis, so if they're wrong and you fail to sell the T-shirts, you'll lose money and be left with dead stock. When pushed, they can't prove any historical sales success for the T-shirts as they're a new line, so what do you do?

One of the options is to offer an official written "contingency contract." It involves upping the stakes for both parties and creating a higher risk deal, so they are forced to "put their money where their mouth is." Often, the other party will back down when you offer this, showing that they don't want to back up their claims. One example of such a contract would be to take the 300 units at £2.50 per unit on the conditions that:

- You will do what you can to sell them: placing them in a prominent position in the shop, using attractive signage to highlight them, as well as preferentially mentioning them to people looking to buy a T-shirt.
- If you *do* sell 300 of them at the rrp of £10 each, as claimed, you will reimburse the supplier with an extra £1.50 per T-shirt. This is an additional 60% revenue for them.
- If you fail to sell 300 of the T-shirts in a prominent position in the store at the rrp of £10 each, the supplier will take back all remaining stock to sell on, at no cost to you.

So, if you sell 300, you make more profit than you usually do and the deal is sweeter for the supplier. If you sell less than 300, you make good profit on those you sell, with no risk to you and the supplier can sell them on to another shop. You get security, your supplier gets reward. The gamble is set in writing and signed by both parties.

Try it

If your counterparts make bold claims that can't easily be substantiated or demand a concession that will cost you, consider upping the stakes of the deal on paper as a contingency contract. Shape it so that each party puts its money where its mouth is and takes a gamble on a higher return.

---

4. Leveraging "Buying Signals"

As persuaders, we're constantly being offered "cues" by our audiences – little signals that indicate an openness, a preference or readiness to accept our offering. In business, you'll often hear these referred to as "buying signals" – an indication that a customer is ready to buy. The previous two techniques both sit comfortably in this category, so perhaps now is a good time to explore it a little more.

The opportunistic beauty of a buying signal is that it gives us a brief window, a moment of power to capitalize on what our audience offers, to convert it into commitment. What's particularly useful is that they flow in abundance during most conversations. The art is to recognize them when they occur, of course. You'll know it's a buying signal when you hear your audience:

* Ask you a question about an aspect of your offering – they're curious to know more;

- Object to what you're saying in any way – they're telling you you're off course and, by definition, hinting at how you can get on course again;
- Make a positive gesture, noise or facial expression after something you say or do – they're indicating that whatever you just said or did works for them.

To leverage buying signals, there are three interchangeable techniques we teach to persuaders. Some work well in certain conditions and less well in other conditions. For example, if someone asks you, "How much is it?" answering their question with a question such as, "How much can you afford?" might come across as a bit wheeler-dealer! The idea is to gain incremental levels of commitment when you hear the signals, so that the final yes comes more easily. They can also be used in conjunction with one another to create some souped-up layered effects. Experiment and see for yourself. The three techniques are as follows:

- Answer a question with a question (AQQ).
- Statement, question (SQ).
- Sharp angle (SA).

So let's run these through some possible questions, objections or signals to show how they might be used.

"What colour do you have these in?"
AQQ: "Is there a particular colour you're looking for?"
SQ: "Red, purple and citron. Which of those would you prefer?"
SA: "If we could persuade the manufacturer to create a bespoke palette for you, would you be happy to order a minimum of 500 today?"
"How long does it take to arrive?"
AQQ: "When do you need it for?"
SQ: "24 hours. Shall I order one for you?"

SA: "Typically five working days but I know that doesn't work for you. If I could get overnight delivery (and I'm not saying I can) would you place the order right now, to expedite that?"

"It's too much!"

AQQ: N\A

SQ: "I see. What's your comparison?"

SA: "If I could move towards you a little on that, would we have an agreement?"

"Ooh!" thumbs up and nodding

AQQ: N/A

SQ: "You like that! How would you use it?"

SA: "Absolutely! If the price is right, would you like to try one?"

Of course, timing is everything (almost . . .), so don't wade in too heavily too early on. I'd recommend you use these sparingly through a conversation and use them right at the close to gain a stronger commitment to action.

 Try it

When you hear your audience ask for more information, object or signal approval, try leveraging the signal by answering their question with a question, using a statement then question or using the sharp angle.

---

5. Assumptive Ask

Using the analogy of the spotlight on the stage, the assumptive Ask positions the question "Do you or don't you?" as out of focus and positions "You've accepted. Now what?" as in focus.

Over the years, I've observed this working best in situations where your audience is lacking in personal confidence or is reluctant to make

STRAIGHT TO YES!

any kind of decision. From a management perspective, it's useful when your audience is procrastinating and needs some strong, directive leadership to move things forward.

The trick here is to imagine they've said, "Yes" to your main request and then imagine what would be the *next things* you'd ask them, to move it along. For example, "What will do you with all of your free time once you've taken this time management course?," "Where would you use this first, out of interest?" and "To which address would you like this delivered?" are all questions that assume the answer to "Shall we go ahead with this?" was "Yes."

If they play nice and answer your question, then you know that you're home and dry. If they object, back off or laugh nervously, take it as feedback that you've some more groundwork to do before popping the question again.

 Try it

Assume your audience has answered in the affirmative to "Shall we go ahead with this?" and ask them a question about the next steps or details needed to move it forward.

---

6. Alternative Choice

I remember the day I uttered an extension of the assumptive Ask and said, "Would you like to go to bed before or after a story?" It was a mini-breakthrough in my parenting skills (not a pick-up line, if that's where you were headed!).

From experience, it takes a very switched-on or wilful individual to set aside the frame that has been offered and create an entirely new frame for discussion. Even in times when my kids initially resisted, I gently persisted with this Ask and they eventually acquiesced, choosing one of the options on the table. It's magic. You can add in as many choices as you like, but two or three choices seem to be most effective.

By giving two or three choices, we create a controlled set of choices, allowing our audience to be in control of, not the whole decision, but a subset of that decision. In other words, instead of a buying frame, "Do I accept or don't I?" it becomes a negotiation frame, "*Which* option am I going for?" What's presupposed here is that we've already decided that you're going for it, it's only the options or details that we need to confirm.

Unsurprisingly, it's a classic sales close in business: don't let that dissuade you from making it a "go to" Ask in your parenting, leadership or fundraising toolkit.

Again, like the assumptive Ask, it's a wonderful question to ask at various times during a persuasive conversation, to narrow down options and increase commitment. Typically, persuaders use it as a conditional, "Would you be more likely to pay with cash or credit card?" or "Which version do you feel more comfortable with: the standard or the deluxe?" "What would be a more affordable start: twenty pounds or five pounds?" Don't overdo it, though! As with any of these Asks, excessive use of one in particular can sound canned and affect your influence attempts.

 Try it

Give your audience two (or perhaps three) choices to focus on that assume they're going for what you're suggesting but give them control over the options.

---

7. How Much is That, Compared to a Cup of Joe?

A cup of coffee is so expensive nowadays, isn't it? We used to pay for one with loose pocket change, now we pay by credit card! While it's perhaps inappropriately priced, the ubiquitous designer cup of coffee offers us a nice persuasion play.

The idea is simple: break down any investment of time or money into a monthly, weekly or even daily figure. You can even spread this over a number of years, if appropriate. An investment of £10,000 over ten years becomes "£1,000 per year, £83 per month, approximately £2.75 per day only – the price of a cup of coffee." Which seems like a better investment: £10,000 or £2.75 per day – the price of a cup of coffee? We all like to pay less, so making your figures small enough to be a "no-brainer" is good practice.

The coffee (or bread, milk, newspaper – in fact any "staple") comparison doesn't work on a time basis, but you could compare it to something mundane. For example, an investment of six hours per month becomes 90 minutes per week, a little over a paltry 12 minutes per day – the time it takes to check and write a couple of emails.

To add to this, recent research on how prices are presented may benefit you, too. Dr Sheryl E. Kimes, Professor at Cornell School of Hotel Administration, led experiments looking at how the presentation of prices affected spend.[1]

The results showed that when the prices appeared on the restaurant menus as $9 or 9 dollars, customers spent less than if the price was presented simply as "9." Again, successful business practitioners back

 Try it

- When presenting an investment, break it down into a very small unit (daily, weekly), which can be compared with a staple good.
- Spell out the price as individual numbers, with no currency types mentioned.

this up instinctively. I've often heard great persuaders present amounts such as £3,420 as, "Three-four-two-zero," no mention of the word "pounds," no mention of any units. It's my belief that this clever practice sidesteps reactance by refocusing us on "small" numbers or perhaps even sidestepping the concept of money entirely.

Ready for Business: A Summary

In this chapter you may have noted that:

- Thinking of what you want as an opportunity for your audience is useful.
- Adopting, "If I could, would you?" is a persuasive reflex.
- When someone makes a bold claim that they can't substantiate, a contingency contract is a useful approach to flush them out or up the stakes and create more value for both sides.
- Responding to buying signals such as questions, facial expressions, your audience touching your products or objections, increases commitment and consistency. You can answer a question with a question (AQQ), use a statement/question (SQ) or the sharp angle (SA).
- When you assume they've said, "Yes!" and confidently ask a question around the next steps, you create a powerful assumptive style of asking.
- Providing two choices to your audience changes the frame from a "Do I or don't I?" internal conversation to a "Which do I?" internal conversation.
- Breaking down a price into a small amount of a month, year or longer and comparing it to a loaf of bread, a cup of coffee or some other staple can make your offer look far more inexpensive.

Now that you have these insights, how might you use some of these approaches to:

- Make something seem inexpensive to a customer?
- Get a colleague excited about your idea?
- Have your family agree to eat out tonight, with minimal dialogue?

In the next chapter you'll garner a fascinating insight into influencing patterns of thinking – yours and theirs.

CHAPTER 6
The Way We See It

In business and life, our patterns of thinking can bring us success, failure or mediocrity. Our brains, in essence, are sophisticated machines that project our deep-rooted expectations onto the screen of life. The old phrase, "We see what we want to see," is very true; as is the phrase, "We see what we don't want to see."

At a deep level, our ingrained and habitual patterns of thinking usually determine how we'll make sense of any given event. Cue "is the glass half empty or half full" conversation.

These expectations and patterns of thinking can empower us and others or limit us when they become no longer fit for purpose. Becoming aware of this, questioning yourself about it and learning how to be mindful of this is something great leaders do well. As is learning how to motivate and liberate others through their unique patterns of thinking.

So, what follows next are some simple, yet deeply satisfying approaches to focus, motivate and unblock patterns of thinking.

1. The Pygmalion Effect

Our expectations influence how people respond to us, as bizarre as that may seem.[1] By definition, other people's expectations influence

The global recession continues to provide a stark and challenging environment for any business, yet many companies continue to grow and prosper in uncertainty. They have effective leaders and salespeople who make maximum impact in every interaction, getting straight to "Yes" and leaving their team, customer or supplier feeling really positive about the experience.

And if you have a product or service that will genuinely benefit that customer, then you owe it to yourself to have the tools necessary to navigate the reasons why not, and get straight to "Yes!" so you achieve the growth that your business deserves.

My favourite approach to dealing with "I can't" is to move them from "glass half empty" to "glass half full" with a few simple questions. "What stops you?" gets them to be specific about the reasons, and "what would happen if you could?" gets them to consider the scenario that you want to get to, after which it seems to them more probable because they have now imagined it as possible.

This is particularly effective when trying to establish who in an organization you should be selling to, because the answers to these questions invariably get you to the decision maker and the budget holder.

**By Matt Hatson, Director Development Projects
at Babcock International Group, plc
http://www.babcockinternational.com**

how we respond to them. It's often referred to as the Pygmalion effect. I don't know about you but I've worked for bosses over the years who made it understood that employees are lazy money hounds, untrustworthy and generally low performers. They were always right. I've had other bosses who made it understood that colleagues will work tirelessly for a cause they believe in, are trustworthy and infinitely capable of high performance. They were always right. Was it just that they were (un)fortunate enough to have the people they had? Or could it be attributed to something more profound in their thinking?

In a wonderful experiment that's been dubbed the Acceptance Prophecy,[2] observers scored test subjects far higher on positive traits when the subjects *expected* to be liked, and far lower when they expected to be rejected.

In Jane Elliot's controversial tests, students who were conditioned to believe they are racially inferior scored very low on spelling tests that day, but when persuaded to believe they were racially superior, scored higher on tests.[3] Our expectations of ourselves and others really can change the game. What are your expectations of yourself and others, when it comes to making requests?

◉ Try it

Having strong, positive, friendly, successful expectations when influencing, leading, goal setting or negotiating will lead to far more positive results. Expect the best.

---

2. Self-Persuasion

"Okay, sell away," said the confident-looking middle-aged man who, with his beautiful wife, sat down in front of a younger me. "You should know, though, that I'm the European Sales Director for Gillette – there's nothing I haven't seen when it comes to sales. And you should also know I'm not buying anything today: this kind of thing just isn't that interesting to me." Rather than arrogant, he was lovely, I thought – playful and charming.

From his opening gambit, I knew I couldn't sell to him but I counted on the fact that he could probably sell to himself quite deftly. After fact-finding and showing him my product, I stuttered and limped through a painful couple of minutes describing features and benefits in the most ungainly way I could before feigning frustration. I said, "Sorry, I'm embarrassed. You're so experienced in this and I'm so new. I'm doing my product and you a real disservice. I'm sure you'd sell these like hot cakes – how would you pitch to me?" He grabbed my pen and pad and with a fire in his eyes began to pitch (very well, in fact) my product to me, presenting the benefits as he saw them. Occasionally, I interjected, "That's brilliant! Why did you pitch that aspect that way?" at which point he'd go even deeper into why it was such an attractive idea. As he finished a few minutes later, I complimented him on his prowess in pitching and added, "OK, so that's it. What do you think? Something you'd like to do?" He and his wife were customers of mine moments later.

Although strong rapport played a part in the sale (we genuinely did get on well) and having his ego stroked weighed in, too, he persuaded himself to buy. Articulating the benefits to me as he saw them was a powerful belief change method and has since been validated in research.[4] Critically, asking them how they'd convince someone else is a very different technique from asking them how they'd convince themselves. Making the target external changes the game, instantly.

◉ Try it

Just before your final request, ask your audience how they would pitch the worthiness of your request to someone else. *Then* ask for their compliance.

3. Hypothetical Frames (WWHTH?)

The trouble with frames is that they're very easy to get stuck in. For many of us, novel experiences diminish in their numbers as we age (seemingly, at least) and we get stuck in habitual patterns of thinking. It's quicker and more energy-efficient than having to renegotiate every moment and proposition from scratch, of course. This phenomenon of "pattern blindness" or "knowing how the story ends" also means that we overlook important nuances in making decisions; nuances that could benefit others and us.

I was working with a designer recently, who, although very talented, polite and intelligent, had become entrenched in certain patterns of thinking. Every time I explained something non-standard that I'd like, he would insist, "We can't do that because . . ." Instinctively, I would come back with my favourite reframing question until I consciously realized this was a pattern and offered it to him as feedback. The question was, "I understand that. So, what would have to happen for it to work?"

It's one of the most extraordinary questions to be asked, because it suddenly liberates your thinking and gives you permission to venture outside of your old frames of reference, in new and exciting ways. Each time, he went away and came back with elegant solutions, some of which delighted him and taught him new things.

Try it

Next time you're faced with immoveable obstacles, try asking, calmly, "I understand that. So, what would have to happen in order to . . . (make it happen/feel comfortable about it/change their minds)?" If they give you certain criteria back, work on delivering those criteria to achieve your outcome! This also now sprinkles on "Consistency": once they've said they'll move ahead based on those criteria, the chances are far higher that they actually will!

The Way We See It: A Summary

In this chapter you may have noted that:

- Your brain projects your non-conscious expectations onto everything and everyone around you.
- Mostly, people see us as we non-consciously expect them to.
- Mostly, people non-consciously behave as they think we expect them to.
- Asking people to convince you or someone else about your offer can have them fall in love with your offer in a big way.
- Asking, "What would have to happen in order to . . . ?" can liberate "stuck" patterns of thinking and give you another route in.

Now that you have these insights, how might you use some of these approaches to:

- Ask someone for something seemingly impossible?
- Have your team start performing to a higher standard?
- Persuade a supplier to extend their payment terms?

Asking with Frames in Mind: A Summary

In this part of the book you've become acquainted with several new ways of inviting people to move your way through subtly shaping their outlook on the situation.

You've learned how to hold your audience accountable to self-image or public declarations, ask small to get the ball rolling and make them work hard to value your offer.

You've picked up knowledge that will have you become a master of creating persuasive contrasts involving fluency, size, immediacy and value. You also learned how to become a rapper and rap a rhyming request as well as picking up some tips about font usage.

I often take the following approach, when making a big board presentation and seeking to gain approval for my recommended course of action.

At the end of the proposal, rather than asking for their comments, I will invite each of the team to comment on what they like in the proposal or how they would improve it further. I do this intentionally to get them thinking positively about the proposal and to engage positively in it. It's often the case that meeting attendees will include the types who look to find fault in proposals or score political points. Getting everyone to make a positive comment tends to redress this. It also has the positive benefit of holding off those keen to throw in random comments because they feel they need to.

Having done this exercise, my experience is that you can then move to a far more constructive and progressive discussion on the proposal.

By a commercial director of a healthcare company

You took stock of some business classics for obtaining the prize: seeing requests as opportunities, conditional requesting ("If I could, would you?") and using a contingency contract to promote honesty and up the stakes. You even picked up some tips for assuming your goal and creating choices as a parent, creating commitment from "buying signals" and comparing prices to a cup of coffee.

Finally, in this section, we looked at projections and expectations, how Pygmalion gets you what you and they expect. How no one can persuade us like we can and how a simple question ("What would have to happen in order to . . . ?") can unlock age-old patterns of thinking.

What next? I love it when you ask that question. Get ready to learn a whole array of techniques that draw upon the very reason the human race is so powerful. In Part Two, you will learn how to become a master of harnessing the rules of tribes . . .

Part Two

Asking with Tribes in Mind

What's Tribes Got to Do with It?

Just for a moment, imagine living in a dystopian, post-apocalyptic, "dog-eat-dog" world, where you can trust no one without significant peril. Resources are scarce. Every man is out for himself. Crime is rife and friendship typically results in betrayal. How do you survive, let alone thrive?

It's a chilling thought, perhaps, because it cuts to the core of what it is to be human. Essentially, as primates, we are pack animals: we can survive in isolation but we only thrive in groups. We seek a pack structure, too: alphas to lead, betas to support and so on. Don't fool yourself into thinking that this doesn't happen – just look at any management team to instantly see it at play.

I believe we need each other to achieve any kind of success and, consequently, there are certain kinds of Ask that tap more directly into our primitive drive to create or maintain social ties and hierarchies. However, by definition, asking anyone for anything is a relatively complex social interaction, often based on the fabulous Technicolor interplay between the quality and nature of the relationships, timings, conditions and psychologies involved. Much of this is beyond our conscious awareness at the moment of asking or being asked.

In other words, just in case you formed the opinion from Part One of this book that pushing a perfect stranger's preset sequence of buttons always results in a positive response, I apologize for that not being the case. People are unique and life, like results, is richer when we create valuable, responsive relationships with family, friends, clients and communities. Developing a mutuality of love, trust, respect, challenge, transparency and listening transforms results and experiences from the boardroom to the bedroom. We're designed to connect, to form tribes and to bond together for strength and security.

Rick van Baaren's research[1] indicates that rapport or "connection" between people (referred to as "mimicry" or "the chameleon effect" in psychology) is our natural default condition. His work highlights how, in the absence of rapport, brain areas associated with disgust and negative affect are active. Mimicry is a signal of social acceptance and, interestingly, viewed using fMRI, triggers similar brain activity to eating chocolate or experiencing romantic love, maternal love and friendship.[2] The impulse to connect, bond, trust, obligate, lead and build support mechanisms is as responsible for creating vibrant, loving communities as it is for driving people to war to protect their kin.

"

We know that people will do things from some emotional states that they wouldn't dream of doing from a different state. So, I use my state, my energy, my words (and questions) and my body language to invite them into a state of creativity, or courage, or determination, or playfulness – and then ask them to make a decision. Provided we're in rapport with the other person, and they trust us, the person with the most congruence and energy will have the most influence.

I've learned several times over the years that if a person is feeling wobbly, anxious or depressed, they're not going to make decisions or take actions in that moment that take them out of their comfort zone! But if I can get them (metaphorically) roaring like a lion, they nearly always amaze themselves and me! It's extraordinary what people are capable of when they feel good about themselves and the world.

By Kimberley Hare, MD, Kaizen Training
www.kaizen-training.com

"

CHAPTER 7
Body Talk

Long before we had words to communicate with, we had a highly sophisticated non-verbal repertoire. Hand gestures, eye movements, tonal variance, posture, facial expressions, lips, tongues, teeth . . . the list is almost endless. Think how a small pre-verbal child communicates and you'll know what I mean.

Putting aside misinterpretations of Albert Mehrabian's research on facial liking, usually starting, "55% of all communication is body language," it's still likely that we pay more attention to non-verbal and environmental data than linguistic data. (For example, we now know that our close primate cousins "sniff" potential partners for dissimilar genetic make-up to maintain genetic diversity.)[1] That said, there are a few words I could say in front of my mother that would still result in a clip across the head, regardless of what body language I was using!

Skilful askers make use of these natural tools to commit their audience in delightful ways, whether through a smile, a touch or the angle of trajectory. What follows is a body of research and examples to help you win the hearts and minds of others when making your request.

1. Right Ear, Right Now

Seasoned negotiators instinctively know that the power seat at the boardroom table is the head of the table facing the entrance to the room. Just as my father's seat was always at the head of our rectangular kitchen table – not something we attempted to change. This is the position where, in tests, we show the lowest stress response: we can see what's coming through the door and have our back to the wall. It's the boss's position that also allows the added benefit of having a "right-hand man," someone we hold in higher esteem than the left-hand man. So, why does the man on the right have the ear of the leader? Research from Daniele Marzoli and Dr Luca Tommasi[2] from the University "Gabriele d'Annunzio" in Chieti, Italy can potentially clarify this.

We know that most people have a dominant hand. You may also know that most people have a dominant eye. You may even be jumping ahead and thinking that people obviously prefer to put a telephone to either their right or left ear . . . but the results and implications, or ear dominance research, in the context of influence and reaching agreement are interesting.

Marzoli and Tommasi's studies show astonishing consistencies around ear preference in communication between humans. Sound entering the right ear is processed preferentially by the left hemisphere, and, for 90% of people, language is usually processed in the left hemisphere. This means that sound entering the right ear hits the language areas immediately. Their research suggests that most people prefer to be addressed in their right ear. Not only that, their experiments show that we are more likely to perform a task when the request hits our right ear rather than our left.

Their experiments were done in nightclubs, of all places, where people often struggle to comprehend what others are saying to them. The three experiments they devised were original and informative.

In experiment one, 286 nightclub-goers were observed talking over loud music. Seventy-two percent of interactions occurred on the right side of the listener.

In experiment two, 160 researchers made a muffled, unintelligible spoken noise in front of the nightclub-goers and waited for the nightclub-goers to offer either their left or right ear to hear properly. The researchers then asked the nightclub-goers for a cigarette: 58%

gave their right ear, 42% gave their left. Women show a marked right-ear preference. Interestingly, no link is established between the number of cigarettes obtained and the ear offered.

In experiment three, cigarettes were requested from 176 nightclub-goers in either their right or their left ear. Significantly more cigarettes were obtained when the request was made in the right ear compared with the left.

According to Marzoli and Tommasi, this confirms "a right ear/left hemisphere advantage for verbal communication and distinctive specialization of the two halves of the brain for approach and avoidance behavior." They suggest that the left hemisphere (right ear) is linked to "approach" behaviour ("do" behaviour), whereas the right hemisphere (left ear) is biased towards "avoidance" behaviour ("don't do"). Perhaps, the trusted "right-hand man" is promoted to our right-hand side for a reason.

 Try it

Think of a request you need to make. What strategies can you come up with to "get on the right side of the other person?"

2. Smile!

"Smile and the world smiles with you" is an old adage with which I wholeheartedly agree. Did you know that the power of the famous yellow smiley face symbol has even been the subject of a fiercely contested lawsuit between retail giant Wal-Mart and *SmileyWorld*, whose licensing of the yellow smiley brand nets them $100,000,000 per year? Wal-Mart companies, such as Asda in the UK, use the smiley face brand to personify their price-reducing policy.

On a domestic note, my wife jokes with me about how I success-fully tempt her to have a cup of tea with me. When I articulate the word "tea" in a normal, neutral, flat way, with my lips hardly moving, she usually declines. However, when I enunciate the word "tea" in a more exaggerated way, so that the vowel is stretched, she typically consents. Try it now in front of a mirror: say "tea" without moving your lips much, then say "tea" and stretch out the vowel. What should actually happen is that, during the second iteration, you appear to be smiling, briefly.

In 2003, Berridge and Winkielman discovered that subliminal exposure to happy, smiling faces has a strong effect on what they term "unconscious emotion" – experienced emotions that influence us but remain out of our awareness. In their studies, thirsty people subliminally exposed to happy faces poured "roughly 50% more of the fruit-flavoured drink into their own cup than if they had seen only neutral facial expressions," and "drank about 50% more of what they poured." By contrast, subliminal angry expressions "caused thirsty participants both to pour less into their cup and to drink less of it than participants primed with subliminal neutral expressions." What's perhaps more interesting is that "thirsty participants reported no conscious awareness of any intervening change in their subjective emotion even when asked before receiving the drink." In other words, it affected them without them knowing.[3]

So what? Now you can persuade people to let you make them a cup of tea? Not quite – there's a wider application here. What it implies is that, for people about to make a decision, your smiling face predisposes them to treat you more favourably.

Over the last 40 years, there have been dozens of studies showing the persuasive power of smiling. For example: smiling waitresses earn more tips,[4] smiling job interviewees create positive impressions[5] and get the job more often[6] and students accused of cheating receive greater leniency when smiling.[7] When we see someone smile, those mirror neurons of ours invite us to smile, too, which influences our emotions and our subsequent behaviour. It's hardwired.

An experiment we sometimes run in workshops is to invite people to place a pencil sideways across their mouth and bite on it, so that they are wearing a smile. We ask them to try their hardest to think of a sad, depressing thought to accompany that expression. Try it yourself, perhaps. Can you feel blue? In similar studies, subjects report finding cartoons funnier with a pencil in this position, compared to subjects holding a pencil in their mouth like a drinking straw, which inhibits the facial muscles involved in smiling. "Facial feedback" works directly on our emotions, not our thinking. But then our emotions work directly on our thinking.[8] Perhaps "Smile and your bank manager smiles with you," is an accurate remix, based on these observations.

Try it

- When you make your request, smile, even though you may be nervous. Make sure photos of you are smiling, especially if they capture a spontaneous, beaming, infectious smile.
- Smile when you speak to people on the telephone: you'll be using a different set of facial muscles that alter the tone of your voice. Your audience will pick up on this and "hear the smile."
- Place images of people (customers, stock photos, team members) smiling on your emails, websites and documents. Even a circular smiley face will do. (I place mine next to the price I'm asking!)
- Use smiling emoticons when you text to help people's emotional interpretation of what you're saying (place the emoticon *before* the statement, to pre-frame what you're about to say).

---

3. A Touching Request

Who would you more readily trust, follow and serve: your partner and children, your boss or a stranger? With whom of these do you have more physical contact?

Typically, when I ask this question of learners in my workshops, it transpires that the more intimate we are with someone, the greater the frequency and duration of physical contact we have with them. Does intimacy trigger physical contact or does physical contact trigger intimacy? Or both? Either way, a wealth of studies shows just how powerful a light touch on the shoulder, elbow or hand can be when looking to win friends and influence people. Even at enterprise level, a common description and strategy consideration for modern organizations is to consider whether they're "hi-tech" or "hi-touch" (or both) as a customer value-creation model. Even though organizations don't *literally* touch us, it communicates their implicit understanding of the power of physical contact to build relationships.

It makes a tangible difference. In studies, researchers asked strangers for directions while touching them and then "accidentally" dropped something straight after. The touched subjects crouched down to help researchers pick up the objects 90% of the time; those strangers who were not touched helped only 63% of the time – a 27% difference.[9]

In another study, test subjects were offered choices: receive a set amount of money or gamble to win more or lose it all. A woman briefly touched one group of subjects on the shoulder as she showed them to their seats. This group chose the high stakes gamble 50% more often.[10]

Jacob Hornik's studies are also fascinating. Waiters and waitresses who touched guests increased tips significantly and also caused

Try it

In any interaction, be sure to touch as many of the people you are interacting with as early as possible. You'll get the best results from a fleeting, one-second touch on the shoulder, elbow or hand. (Handshakes help but do not count towards this.) Even an accidental "brush" across the hand has been proven to increase responsiveness.

customers to evaluate the restaurant more favourably. He also found this in retail store settings: a brief touch led to increases in customers' shopping times, evaluations and spend.[11]

4. The Eyes Have It

"Eyes are the window to the soul," is a wonderful metaphor to explain how a certain kind of eye contact can disarm us and promote honesty and compliance. West Midlands Police in the UK used the following research in a well-publicized seasonal crime prevention initiative that led to them writing in their official report, "(Operation Momentum) achieved excellent results." Furthermore, beggars who establish eye contact with strangers when asking for money are more likely to receive it.[12]

Melissa Bateson's research at the University of Newcastle showed how prolonged eye contact can bring about higher levels of honesty or accountability in the person being "stared" at, even when we're stared at by a picture of an eye. An A5 poster was placed above an honesty box in a university cafeteria. It showed prices of tea, coffee and milk and featured an image that was changed each week, from different pictures of flowers to different images of eyes, staring directly at the onlooker. The study showed that, on average, students put 2.76 times as much into the honesty box on the weeks when the poster featured pictures of eyes.[13]

Kellerman, Lewis and Laird documented what we already know: that gazing into the eyes of others significantly increases feelings of passionate love, dispositional love and liking.[14] Fry and Smith showed how, in a face-to-face context, mutual gaze facilitates the encoding and recall of information.[15]

At the University of Aberdeen, several hundred students rated nearly identical photos of computer-generated faces with smiling or disgusted expressions on two factors: sexual attractiveness and like-ability. The only difference in each pair of photos was that in one image the irises pointed straight at the viewer; in the other they pointed off to the side. Both men and women rated faces looking straight at them higher on attraction and likeability, even when the faces wore expressions of disgust. The studies even held true for students from Asian cultures, where direct gaze is often a sign of disrespect (although it was noted that this displayed a private preference, not a public one).[16]

Try it

When asking for honesty, keep a positive intention for your audience and hold eye contact with them as you go for it and after you ask. Even if they look away, be there for them when they reestablish eye contact. Hold it until they make a decision either way.

5. Up Close and Personal

Earlier, I suggested that "intimacy breeds trust breeds influence." So, do all behaviours associated with intimacy increase influence? Perhaps, perhaps not. However, the field of proxemics – the study of how we perceive and use "intimate, personal, social and public space"[17] while responding to non-conscious and cultural cues – presents us with some interesting clues.

Picture the scene: diners in a cafeteria are approached by an experimenter who asks them to volunteer for one of two surveys – 30 minutes or two and a half hours. What's unknown to the diner is that the experimenter is making the request either 12 to 18 inches away, deemed close enough to violate the diner's personal space, or three to four feet away – a safer distance. The results of the study are clear-cut – diners volunteer for longer surveys when the distance between them and the requester is smaller.[18]

 Try it

When you make your request, get up close and personal.

In more recent studies, we also see the same effect at play. For example, when a waitress takes an order while standing closer to a diner, the frequency of tips increases, as does the size of the tip. Waitresses saw increases of 22.6% by standing 0.6 metres closer to guests (0.15 m away versus 0.75 m).[19]

Proximity, it seems, begets intimacy, begets influence.

 Try it

While there's no research to support the following suggestion, I'd recommend slightly increasing your font size when making your request in writing, to mimic the effect of moving closer.

---

6. The Outstretched Hand

It's said that Warren Buffett, CEO of Berkshire Hathaway, negotiated the acquisition of McLane Distribution (a $23 billion enterprise) from Wal-Mart with one two-hour meeting and a handshake. Usually, a merger of this size would take several months to complete and cost several million dollars to pay for an entourage of legal and financial experts. But in this instance, it completed in less than a month.

The power of the handshake is implicitly understood the world over and in many cultures, such as Asia and the Middle East, it is far more binding than the written contracts we fuss over in the western hemisphere. A handshake signals trust, partnership, affiliation and shared goals. Imagine then, you make eye contact with your audience and hold out your hand to shake on the deal and their hands remain firmly on the table at which they're sitting. You've been rebuffed, spurned, rejected. The rapport is broken. There's a terrible silence. When you *figuratively* feel isolated, you *literally* feel the temperature drop in the room.[20]

Such is the implicit understanding of what it means to knock back an attempted handshake, that the pain of doing so is virtually unbearable for two people in some kind of agreement. Over the years, I've seen countless deals closed non-verbally with a simple smile, locking in of the eyes and an outstretched hand. It's a call and response that brings home the bacon.

◎ Try it

When it's time to make your request, smile, gain eye contact and confidently extend your hand, like you expect a handshake to happen.

---

7. Down with Credibility

Increasingly, it seems, UK and Ireland contact centres are located in places such as Newcastle, Liverpool, Cork or Glasgow where the local accent has a wider modulation in pitch than other regions, often rising at the end of the sentence. Callers often talk about how they love the accents and how people from these regions are so friendly. It could also be that these areas, being less economically prosperous, offer certain taxation advantages for companies. Or both. Or neither.

Interestingly, though, there are two main vocal pitch changes in the animal kingdom, each having a different function. The first change is where our pitch lifts at the end of a sentence. Think Australian accents

("G'day, mate!"), LA "Valley girl" accents ("This one time, at band-camp . . ."). A rising pitch at the end of a sentence signals a question or invitation to another to comment, approve or join in. It's cooperative, inclusive, friendly and even submissive.

The second change is where our pitch drops at the end of a sentence (think the bass line from Queen's *Under Pressure* or Vanilla Ice's *Ice Ice Baby*). Amongst primates, this is received as a command, an order, an instruction to comply with. It's dominant and authoritative. If you own a dog, you'll probably recognize that dogs also respond to this drop in pitch at the end of a sentence.

Barack Obama is a great exponent of this. If you watch or listen to his speeches, you'll hear these same beautiful cadences in his Southern-Baptist influenced style. His voice pitch soars, glides and drops at the end of a phrase, gently bringing us back down to earth after sailing through the skies with him.

Counterintuitively, great persuaders *drop* their voice pitch when making a request, even though they still want their audience to respond. While the syntax of their words suggests a question, the non-verbal message is, "comply." The falling pitch conveys credibility, power, gravitas and confidence rather than the rising pitch's message of invitation, indecision and harmony.

 Try it

Practise dropping your voice pitch as you end your request, like Barack Obama.

---

8. Smooth Talker

Several times during my life I've been labelled a "smooth talker" by friends, colleagues and clients and always wondered what that meant, in practice. Do you happen to know a smooth talker? Does it mean they're good at appreciating you and giving compliments? At understanding what you need in the moment and reframing ideas? At presenting a vivid vision of the future and making it painless to take a first step? Or just that they have the "gift of the gab," perhaps?

Maybe it's all of those, but one thing I discovered with great fascination was that the fluency and speed at which we speak has a noticeable effect on how credible and persuasive we are in the eyes and ears of others. Put simply, speaking more quickly lends us more credibility.[21]

Think of when you've seen an auctioneer perform, listened to radio advertising, watched a market trader at work: every one of those speakers talks in a fast and fluent way. Fast talkers are just more convincing.

A more recent study, however, adds a wonderful nuance to the debate that instantly made sense to me. Smith and Shaffer's research found that faster talking is more persuasive when people are *not yet* convinced by you; slower talking is more persuasive when your audience agrees with you. This holds true when we think of Martin Luther King's "I have a dream" speech, for example, celebrated as one of the greatest speeches of all time. MLK speaks to an audience that mostly adores him and trusts him as their leader. His speech is measured, slow and full of pauses. Contrast this to the pitch of the market trader, trying to catch your attention quickly and persuade you that you need what they have to offer, even though you've seen their wares and have continued on your business.[22]

 Try it

If you sense your audience doesn't fully agree with you yet, speak more quickly. If you sense that your audience agrees with you, slow down.

Body Talk: A Summary

In this chapter you may have noted that:

- The way you use you body can have as much (or greater) influence on your outcomes as your words.
- Your right ear may be more open to persuasion.
- A genuine smile, which includes wrinkling the eyes, works wonders on people.
- Briefly touching someone endears you to them and often causes riskier behaviour.
- Eye contact promotes greater emotional connection and honesty.
- The closer you are when you ask, the more successful the result.
- An outstretched hand is painful to rebuff.
- Dropping your voice pitch at the end of a sentence lends you credibility.
- Speaking quickly convinces the yet-to-be-convinced; speaking slowly further convinces the already convinced.

Now that you have these insights, how might you use some of these approaches to:

- Encourage a direct report to be more honest during a high-stakes conversation?
- Create a feeling of intimacy as you ask your friend for a favour?
- Signal to a cold caller that the conversation is now over?

In the next chapter you'll learn quick and simple ways not only to get your result but also to build better relationships as you make that all-important request.

CHAPTER 8
The Name's Bond . . . Social Bond

An emerging trend in multinational organizations' customer service strategies can be expressed simply in two words – "personalization" and "connection." There's a growing focus on how, as organizations, they can bring the customer's life into their business (personal data mining), bring their business into their customer's life (social networking) and tailor key aspects of the product, service or experience to each customer. How they can connect more often in more meaningful ways with customers. How they can become beloved by the customer, make each touch-point more authentic and enjoy a long-term bond together.

Bonding with each other is what we're programmed to do. One of our deepest fears is that we may end up alone; being alone long term can be a predictor of "failure to thrive" syndrome in adults, which can lead to an early grave.

Big business has realized that profit is also about relationships. Just as strong family relationships are based on experiences of love, trust, humility, patience, learning, fun, challenge and accountability, so too can B2B or B2C relationships be.

What follows is a collection of approaches that tap into and develop your social bonds, either face to face, through your marketing or through your customer service efforts.

For me, influence is about trust. The word "trust" is the hardest word in the English language to realize but you can get there by being consistent, respectful and patient. It's a very Japanese thing: we're not wild about conflict, though we'll do it if we have to. Instead we influence by being scrupulously respectful.

We have complex relationships with strategic landlords, such as Selfridges, Harvey Nichols, House of Fraser and the airports: these are very sensitive relationships and you have to be aware that somebody else is hosting you in their environment, they are not just landlords. It's a partnership, a marriage: you have to work at it, with the unavoidable ups and downs along the way. So, we play the long game with landlords, banks, employees and contractors, understanding their point of view, their goals and their constraints by putting ourselves in their shoes. They value us being open communicators, rather than being overly hard-nosed.

I've always been a great exponent of "the seven meeting rule": by being utterly charming and consistent, you get to the point where you actually sometimes wear people down, they acquiesce and agree to very acceptable terms!

By Robin Rowland, CEO, Yo! Sushi www.yosushi.com

1. Give First, Ask Later

The social phenomenon psychologists refer to as reciprocity is a powerful and fascinating thing. Imagine doing someone you know a favour: perhaps you lend him or her money when they are in a fix, proactively introduce them to their future wife or help them paint their new house, for example. Maybe you could term what you did as "beyond the call of duty," "adding value" or "an act of friendship or love."

Now imagine that you'd like their help in the form of a ride to and from the airport for your summer holiday, so you don't have to pay hundreds for parking. You ask them and they start to make excuses and wriggle out of it. You know they're free on those dates and can do it but don't want to do it. How do you feel? How do you feel about them? How do you feel about the balance of your relationship with them?

Most of us would entertain thoughts somewhere along the continuum of, "That's odd – I thought we had that kind of relationship," to, "Unbelievable! How out of order is that? The things I've done for them!" In this scenario, the rule of reciprocity has been broken.

Reciprocity "makes social exchange possible by allowing one person to initiate giving without fear of losing the initial 'investment.'"[1] It's a way of creating obligations to each other that make it likely that we continue to look out for each other in our tribes. An implicit code of "If you scratch my back, I'll scratch yours. Maybe not today. Maybe not tomorrow. But someday."

It's the reason why savvy charities send out pens and other gifts with their letters, asking for donations. Rather than offering a gift in exchange for a donation, they know that if they give a "free" gift first, the odds of the recipient putting their hand in their pocket increase considerably. In one study, roughly 10,000 donation request letters were sent to potential donors. One third of the letters contained no gift, one third contained a small gift (one postcard plus one envelope) and the final third contained a large gift (four postcards plus four envelopes). The likelihood of donations increased by 17% where the small gift was included but increased by 75% where the large gift was included.[2]

An eye-opening study by Dennis Regan from 1971 shows us another example of how this process works in the real world. Researchers created an "aesthetic enjoyment" experiment for students at Stanford University, who received a whopping $1.75 each to take part. The experiment was designed to measure the effect of liking and favours on compliance. Test subjects took part in pairs: one an unwitting test subject, the other a confederate (in other words "in" on the experiment).

The experiment manipulated the real test subject into either liking or disliking the confederate before the "art appreciation study" began. During a brief pause between rounds, the confederate slipped out and returned with either two bottles of Coca-Cola or nothing. In the version where they returned with two Cokes, the confederate explained to the other student that they'd asked the experimenter whether or not he or she could buy a Coke: when told yes, they explained how they bought one for the other student also. In other words, the confederate had done them an unexpected favour.

After another round of art appreciation, the confederate slipped the real test subject a note, saying, "Would you do me a favour? I'm selling raffle tickets for my high school back home to build a new gym. The tickets cost ¢25 each and the prize is a new Corvette. The thing is, if I sell the most tickets I get 50 bucks and I could use it. If you'd buy any, would you just write the number on this note and give it back to me right away so I can make out the tickets? Any would help, the more the better. Thanks." This was the primary measure of the experiment: the quantity of raffle tickets sold.

The results? Even in conditions where the real test subject reported disliking the confederate, the simple Coke favour nearly doubled the average number of tickets bought and more than doubled the proportion of the subjects buying more than a single ticket, raising this proportion from 25% in the two control conditions to 58% in the favour condition. The researchers also claimed that the simple act of receiving and returning a favour led the test subjects to rate themselves as liking the confederate more compared to those who did not receive a favour.[3]

One distinction here is that the power of the exchange lies not in a conditional "If you give me this, I'll give you that" frame, where your gift is contingent on their compliance, but rather a "Since I've been good to you, will you be good to me?" frame, where the exchanges don't necessarily seem connected.

A second distinction is possibly the difference that makes the difference for harnessing the power of reciprocity. For people to understand that you have done something generous for them that they ought one day to repay, your deed needs to be labelled as something generous. For example, imagine an employee approaches you and asks for an early finish on Friday. Being a kindly soul, you say you'll look into it and get back to them. Later that day, you come back to them and say that it's possible and you've authorized it. They thank you. You politely reply, "It's all right/you're welcome/don't worry about it/my pleasure/no, it's cool," or something similarly courteous and dismissive.

Right there, just by being polite, you've significantly reduced the chances of them ever repaying the favour or even recognizing it as a favour to be repaid. Because some people with whom you interact will see this as standard issue, an entitlement that they can also expect next time. After all, it was so easy for you to do it, seemingly. And when you have to refuse them next time they ask, they pull a face, complain and gripe to others about how unfair or inflexible you are. Can you recognize this, perhaps with a child or partner, rather than an employee?

In relationships where a mutuality of love, trust, care, attention, respect or value-creation does not exist, you absolutely must "label" all acts of giving for reciprocity. This will communicate to the other party that you're going above and beyond the call of duty. That what you are doing is anything other than standard. That it took extra time, thought, influence, energy, money or trust on your part. Only when people understand the effortful essence of your deed will they feel indebted to you. Importantly, your "give" should be of a similar perceived value to the "get" you're aiming for. In other words, don't give a mint and expect to get a Mercedes.

Try it

- Before asking for anything, think about what you can give first, as a generous and unexpected favour or treat. This could be in the form of time, money, information, compliments, introductions, kindness, support or energy, as examples.
- When someone thanks you for something you have put valuable resources into, avoid dismissing their thanks and instead "label" it for reciprocity by saying something like, "You'd do the same for me, I'm sure," or, "We're a team. I'd like to think that's what we do for each other when needed," or even, with a smile in your eyes, "Well, you do realize that means you now owe me your first-born, right?"

2. "Don't Feel Obliged"

Why do so many businesses offer a first step that has no obligation to follow up? And not just small direct sales organizations that sell windows or insurance, we're talking companies that turn over hundreds of millions of dollars per year such as Sophos or Disney Vacations. Is it just that they're generous? Perhaps. Is it that they can get you to take a small step towards them and start the consistency and commitment process, outlined in Part One of this book? Potentially. Is it so they can capture your details to market to you? Could be. It could also be that, for many people, even just the mention of the social codes of reciprocity, duty or obligation initiates those processes.

Although there's no research I've come across to quantify how and why this works, I've found in my business activities that, with some people, merely *referencing* obligation increases responsiveness instantly.

For example, you're having a party and you say to a friend, "It's on Saturday at 7pm – don't feel obliged to bring a bottle or anything," what you're in fact doing is subtly suggesting that there's an *expectation* that they'll bring a bottle, if not an obligation. Thinking about this social code tends to evoke the feelings associated with the social code and the accompanying behaviours usually ensue.

Other examples might be:

"There's no obligation, you understand, but it'd be useful for you to attend the meeting at 4pm."

"Please don't feel obliged, but I'm asking for a small donation for the charity I support and even a penny would help if you can afford it."

Starting of your request with, "Don't feel obliged to accept, but . . ." prepares your audience for reciprocity before you even make your request.

Of course, you'll appreciate that this works best in balanced relationships where you create value for each other and the other person feels they owe a debt to you in some way. In other words, it may not work so well with teenagers . . .

Incidentally, asking someone not to think about something is effectively an instruction to think about it. For example,

Don't think of the sound of a bell ringing . . .

Did you hear the sound of a bell ringing, however fleetingly? If you did, case closed. (If you didn't, certainly don't think of a slice of hot apple pie with vanilla ice cream slowly melting all over it.)

Try it

Try peppering some of your requests with, "Don't feel obliged, but . . ." before you pop the question because you'll tap in to obligation and reciprocity.

---

3. Flattery

"Flattery will get you nowhere," goes the old adage. Well, maybe it's time to scrap that one. If it's good enough for ultra-savvy marketers at Coca-Cola that know the power of flattery, it's good enough for me. In fact, Coca-Cola recently flattered an entire continent to ramp up sales of its burpy beverage there (search for "A billion reasons to believe in Africa" on YouTube to see the fruits of their labour).

Backing it up, researchers Elaine Chan and Jaideep Sengupta, who define flattery as "communicating positive things about another person without regard to that person's true qualities or abilities" ran studies in 2010 that showed that test subjects who were exposed to flattery from a mailshot from fictitious company PerfectStore reacted in a counterintuitive way.

The PerfectStore mailshot included the text, "We are contacting you directly because we know that you are a fashionable and stylish person. Your dress sense is not only classy but also chic. As someone with exceptional taste in clothes, you will enjoy the designs featured in our new collection, featuring 'must-haves' for the coming season."

Test subjects then underwent a series of questions and tests based on the mailshot and returned to do more tests three days later. The observation was that even though 76% of the students consciously saw the text as "flattery with an ulterior motive" and the leaflet as "aimed at persuading them to buy PerfectStore's products" they still retained very positive feelings towards PerfectStore days later.

Even when the fakery is forgotten, the favourable feeling stays.[4]

So, if flattery works, even though we know it's a persuasion play, imagine how far appropriate, sincere appreciation can extend your influence. For example,

"You've a critic's eye: it's obvious you really know what you're looking for. Which one can you see yourself living with, long term?"

"You always make such delicious puddings, first name, any chance you could bring one to my party on Saturday?"

"First name, there are people that know and there are people that don't know. You strike me as someone that knows and I think you know that this is a perfect fit for your portfolio. Do you see that?"

"I've seldom encountered anyone as consistently generous as you, first name, truly. And I'm hoping I can count on your generosity to support us with this tonight. Will you back us when the time comes?"

Try it

Use sincere compliments when making your written or verbal requests, to amplify your audience's positive feelings towards you.

---

4. Ask for Trust

Perhaps in a similar way to asking for obligation, asking specifically for trust can lend a powerful boost to your cause. The old phrase, "Trust me, I'm a doctor," springs to mind as a way for medical professionals to perform highly personal manoeuvres with patients. Jimmy Carter emerged from the relative obscurity of a peanut farm in his native Georgia to run for the US presidency, appealing to voters, and winning, with his slogan "Trust me."

Similarly, in a 2006 study, researchers found that communicating a message that you can be trusted boosted a whole range of measures in surveys: value for money, caring, fair treatment, quality and competency. In the study, the quality and competency perceptions for an auto services firm were both boosted by 30% or more through using the phrase, "You can trust us to do the job for you," at the end of an advert.

In *The Moral Molecule*, researcher Paul "Dr Love" Zak talks about the neurochemical oxytocin, the trust chemical. Oxytocin decreases our anxiety around strangers and encourages us to act in pro-social ways, to facilitate stronger social ties. In trials, a good squirt of it up your nose will have you being more generous with money and spraying it into a room causes people spontaneously to start hugging. Zak has shown how, for 98% of people, pro-social acts trigger an increase in oxytocin, resulting in an increase in trust and connection. The other 2% he affectionately labels "bastards;" people who are wired differently and don't respond to kindness by experiencing a rush of oxytocin.[5]

Perhaps the acts of touching people, complimenting then, gifting them and trusting them all result in an oxytocin squirt or two. In any case, letting people know that they can trust you is an ancient signal that can work wonders in your persuasion attempts, as long as you deliver on your promise.[6]

 Try it

- In your requests, remind people that they can trust you, your organization or your offering to deliver on your promise. Make sure that you can deliver on it.
- Shortly before asking for something, show people that you trust them in some way. You could disclose some personal information about yourself, allow them to make decisions without having to consult you or allow them access to more confidential material or ideas.

---

5. Swap Trumpets

I have the good fortune to coach some very talented executives. They're generally committed to professionalism, growth, ethics, respect and responsibility. They achieve strong results. Consistently, however, their humility disbars them from promoting their own successes to their bosses, peers or direct reports: "That would be blowing my own trumpet," is the frequent response to my asking them who else knows about the successes they've just shared with me. All a bit vulgar for their refined sensibilities.

It's a catch 22. If you achieve the success, but don't promote it, who will know? How will that affect your standing in your group or organization? If you promote your success, will people label you a ladder-climber, narcissist or egomaniac? How will that affect your standing in your group or organization? Apparently, you're damned if you do; damned if you don't.

There is a remedy for this, however, in two flavours. What people don't seem to mind is someone else blowing your trumpet for you. Imagine we're on the same team and, during a meeting, a colleague says, "Guys, can I just take a minute to share some good news? I don't know if you've heard but Haider's achieved some really strong results this quarter on the Borneo programme – a 13% uplift compared to last quarter. I just wanted to recognize how significant that is and maybe ask him for a bit more detail on what he's been doing that's different. Haider?"

Do you think that I'm arrogant? Self-promoting? Hopefully not – it wasn't me who brought it up. All you need to do is to identify a couple of people in your team that you trust to be your cheerleaders and contract with them that you'll blow each other's trumpets. Packaging your request as an opportunity for them to get the recognition they deserve is a good way to do this.

Taking it a stage further, you could harness the power of reciprocity and become the person who notices and celebrates other people's successes. Doing so exponentially increases the chance that others will do this for you. As Gandhi famously said, "You must be the change you wish to see."

Please note, there is a clear and present danger associated with this one: namely, that everyone in your team starts doing it, sharing and celebrating each other's successes. Before you know it, you've fallen into the trap of becoming a communicative, close-knit, supportive team. Beware!

Try it

Ask someone else to blow your trumpet and, in exchange, blow his or hers. Be humble, subtle and natural about it, as if it was unexpected.

1. Have your cheerleader learn the specifics of the success and recount it in its entirety in front of the group. If the story around your success is complicated, avoid this one and choose option two instead. Do the same for them next time.
2. Ask your cheerleader to announce the general theme of the success then invite you to share more of the details. Do the same for them next time.

The Name's Bond . . . Social Bond: A Summary

In this chapter you may have noted that:

- Forming small tribes, personal links and bonds is hardwired into our make-up.
- Giving *before* asking makes your requests more successful: more so when it's seen as unrelated to your request; less so when it's framed as, "I'll trade you 'x' for 'y.'"
- People will reciprocate the size or value of what you give: give more, get more.
- Just mentioning obligation will prime most people for acts of giving and agreeing.
- Flattery gets you somewhere, even when it's seen as fake.
- Acts of trust and kindness release oxytocin, the love hormone, in you and your audience. When you show someone you trust him or her, they bond to you.

- Reminding someone they can trust you to do a good job is very persuasive, if you have a good track record of making good on your word.
- People aren't offended if someone else blows your trumpet and asks you to expand.

Now that you have these insights, how might you use some of these approaches to:

- Arouse in your customer a sense of obligation before the crunch meeting?
- Promote your results in the workplace without being seen as arrogant?
- Initiate reciprocity when your backers thank you for helping them out?

In the next chapter you'll learn fascinating and practical approaches to leveraging some well-hidden social rules that move people your way, fast.

CHAPTER 9
The Wider Tribe

Let's face it, the only reason we're still here may be because we learned to thrive together in small groups. Studies show the entire human race dwindled to about 2,000 people in total around 150,000 years ago. That's all: imagine a tiny section of a football stadium. As a species, it's thought we would have faced extinction had the harsh climactic conditions continued much longer. At that point, we split into small communities for the next 100,000 years before reuniting with separate genetic lineages and beginning our migratory journeys out of Africa. Small tribes give us the conditions to thrive and prosper, even despite a harsh external environment. British anthropologist Robin Dunbar even goes as far as to say that the maximum tribe size we can effectively handle is between 100 and 230 people ("Dunbar's number" is commonly cited as 150 people).[1]

Muzafer Sherif's famous "Robber's Cave" experiments in the 1950s[2] showed that a group that has an awareness of other groups existing begins to attribute positive qualities to itself (the "in-group") and negative traits to those other groups (the "out-groups"). It makes sense. Evolving this way would serve to keep members within the group, help the group thrive, feel confident and fend off other groups who might capture their resources.

So, it seems we're hardwired for tribes – another way of saying groups or communities. And that hardwiring plays out very

These days one of our most precious commodities is time. This means that, as leaders, we have to find ways for people to stay focused and get things done quickly and efficiently, whilst staying aligned to strategy.

The best way for leaders to get the best out of their people in this way, in my view, is to set out a crystal clear view of the organization's vision and values. A clear, purposeful vision gives people a framework of reference and a means to work out, for themselves, what to do. To be effective, though, the vision needs to be engaging, real and differentiated. Banal, anodyne, "motherhood and apple pie" wording won't cut it.

Well-articulated and resonant values, lived and breathed by senior leadership with total commitment, help people to work out how to get stuff done without having to refer back to the leader.

Persuading people is best done, in my view, and perhaps paradoxically, by giving people freedom to make their own decisions, yet within a clear framework of vision and values.

By Paul Stobart, CEO CPP Group plc www.cpp.co.uk

significantly in the art and science of influence: we more readily follow and trust our tribe's opinion and welcome those into our tribe if we think they are like us. "Like us" could mean they look and talk like us, hold the same beliefs and values as us or have the same vision, mission or goals as us. Pulling on those ties, within your tribes, becoming part of your audience's tribe and inviting them into yours is where the power of the modern world now lies.

What follows is a group of approaches that relate to making persuasive requests that tap into your social bonds.

1. Herd Mentality

When I was a teenager, growing up in Newcastle-upon-Tyne, my friends and I used to play a devilish game in town on Saturday afternoons. Maybe you've played it before yourself?

We'd stand in a group of four or more, staring up at a fixed point in the sky, as if mesmerized by an insanely absorbing drama waiting to unfold. We'd occasionally nudge each other and whisper something, to add to the drama. If anyone asked us, "What's going on?" we'd reply, "Just watch and wait . . ." and resume our gaze.

On a good day, curious people would assemble to see what was happening and, gradually, a small crowd would usually form around us. The larger the crowd became, the more people were attracted to join the crowd. At a certain size, we would gradually slip away, one at a time, to gleefully observe the crowd from the other side of the main square. One day we reached a crowd of nearly twenty people, all staring up at the sky and not knowing why, waiting for something mysterious but not knowing what. If you were one of them, my apologies: it was, ahem, "research."

"Social proof" or "consensus" is the concept of safety in numbers, sometimes referred to as the "magnetic middle," "herd mentality" or "sheep factor." Think about it: the crowd has the strength, breadth of experience and collective wisdom to guide us and so we are programmed to go with that crowd without thinking. Most of us. By ourselves, our chances of finding food, shelter and a mate start to dwindle. A crowd or tribe also allows us to share the decision-making burden, saving precious mental energy, although sometimes with disastrous results known as the "bystander effect" or "diffusion of responsibility."[3]

Examples in business and media abound: "eight out of ten cats prefer Whiskas" cat food, we're told; YouTube's view counter; Zumba adverts featuring well-toned testimonial after well-toned testimonial; restaurants marking items on their menu as "our most popular items;" canned laughter on TV. TripAdvisor noted that people who see content from their friends on TripAdvisor contribute personal content to the site at double the rate of others and are 20% more engaged than other users.

A great example of using the crowd to persuade is the wonderful Avaaz.org – "a global civic organization that promotes activism on issues such as climate change, human rights, corruption, poverty and conflict" (Wikipedia). Avaaz wants visitors to sign online petitions that are then sent to key members of governments around the world.

On the home page, the ever-increasing ticker shows you how many people like you have joined the cause: "THE AVAAZ MOVE-MENT: 14,609,673 members worldwide." Visit them to see the huge numbers of people taking action on issues that matter. As well as a compelling message, they have a constant stream of names of people like you who've just signed the petition under a "Happening Right Now" section. Seeing numbers showing that millions of people have petitioned, seeing the politicians endorsing their cause with testimonials and seeing the stream of new people adding their support makes for an incredibly persuasive call to action. We feel compelled to move in their direction.

Have you ever noticed how some people are really generous to buskers by putting large notes in? Who puts a twenty-pound note in a guitar case in real life? Probably the busker. They know we're far more likely to give and give generously if we see that many people have given before us and "given large." Filling the "coin jar" before you start asking for donations shows passersby that your cause is worth giving to. That's partly why they shake the collection bucket: not just to get your attention, but also to show that others like you are giving. Even hearing others laugh in the form of canned laughter is proven to make us rate television programmes as funnier than without the canned laughter.

So, the use of social proof is extremely persuasive, especially when that proof is from people with whom your audience identifies (for example, the same age, ethnicity, hobbies, social status, gender, sexual orientation, profession, union, etc.) or from people whom your audience admires.

Try it

- Find a way to show your audience that the majority of their family, friendship circle, team, division, company, industry, neighbourhood, special interest group or demographic is already convinced and moving your way. High percentages (greater than 60%), testimonials, celebrity, manager or expert endorsements and signatures are all great ways to show this.
- Create a petition. Once you've amassed a large amount of names, use it or keep it visible to show just how popular your cause is.
- Fill the bucket with change and shake it as people pass by, so they hear how much people have contributed already. Put some notes in the bucket, too, so they see how much people are giving.
- In a group setting, ask members of the group who have already decided to move your way to stand up and share why.

---

2. Affiliation and Aspiration

One of the great persuasion trends across the Internet of recent years was started, I believe, by Facebook. On certain sites that you visit, you may notice that the website or article indicates how many of your friends have "liked" this page on Facebook or Google+. It even shows you specifically who from your tribe likes it. Once we see that several members of our community have liked something, our curiosity is more likely to be piqued. After all, if the tribe's talking about it, I don't want to be left out – it might be useful.

We are influenced by those to whom we relate. An heuristic that launched an entirely new industry – the celebrity perfume. Stars such as Jennifer Lopez and Beyoncé have become aspirational brands: admiring their style, their work and what they stand for means we're more likely to buy into the person, emulate their choices and accept their recommendations for how we smell, dance or dress. For example, I loved rock bands when I was a teenager, so I grew my hair long. Not a good look for me but a common example of affiliation.

In short, we like to be like the people we like or would *like* to be like. Maybe read that sentence again. Unless you've just re-read it – escape the loop now!

A proven approach that more retailers use is crowd-sourced preferences. Spotify has its "What your friends are listening to now" feature and visibility of that on Facebook. iTunes has its "Genius" feature, Amazon has its "People who bought this, also went on to buy this," emails. All of these approaches aim to connect you to add-ons that people like you are adding on.

Try it

Provide examples of people with whom your audience affiliates (same clubs, street, race, special interest group, family) or aspires to be like (the boss, business guru, musician, actor) whose thinking aligns with your suggestion or who have already given you their commitment or support.

3. Social Taboo

A taboo is a practice that is prohibited, restricted or not allowed to be uttered, according to the norms of a tribe. "It's not the done thing," as the Queen of England might say. Incest might be one shocking example of this; however, there are many smaller daily taboos that we feel uncomfortable around, which can be used in persuasive requests.

I was at work, meeting with my boss and colleagues one day a while back. I'd been nominated for a prestigious national award and had to travel to London for the swanky ceremony. My boss announced that there was an extra place available, paid for by the company. Most of the team really wanted to go, we got on very well indeed and it promised to be a great party, regardless of the outcome. Yet, one particular colleague desperately wanted to go partying and she came out with the classic line,

"I really want to go. Would anyone object if it was me?"

All around the table was an awkward silence . . . How, as polite, nurturing people could they object to someone going to celebrate with me? There was a moment's discomfort and, seething in the most passive–aggressive British way, they hesitantly began to say, "Err, no. That's fine."

My winning colleague had tapped into social norms around "enabling people," and "being a supportive team" that seven leaders around

---

Try it

If you're in a group of people, jostling for position and want to put yourself forward, try airing this, "I'd love to. Would anyone object if it were me?"

the table were reluctant to break. Of course, all they had to do was repeat the same line to open the conversation back up again (but hindsight is a gift, as they say). I won the award and she burned up the dance floor like a true disco diva 'til two in the morning. I was glad she asked.

4. Authority and Insider Knowledge

Growing up as one of four siblings, I became accustomed to a two-step persuasion play that went something like this:

Sibling: "You have to let me have a go . . . NOW."
Me: "No. I don't."
Sibling: "Dad says."
Me: "*Aargh*. OK, then."

Implicit here is the understanding that breaking with authority carries consequences and that by flaunting someone else's authority, we validate our own position. However, as you'll read in Chapter 17, using certain people's authority can undermine your persuasion plays in the long term.

One group that is not only safe to use, but advantageous is the expert. Since the earliest examples of society, elders, shaman, oracles and other visionaries have been lionized and sought out for their seemingly otherworldly gift, often paid for in blood. We ache for their insight to help inform our decision making.

In fact, nowadays, markets can rise or fall based on the expertise or insider knowledge of certain "inseers." Take the example of Robert Peston, journalist and reporter for the BBC. From *Wikipedia*,

"While no impropriety on the part of Peston was implied, it was claimed in *The Observer* on 19 October 2008 that the Serious Fraud Office (SFO) could enquire into the source of one of Peston's scoops, which, in September 2008 in the fraught atmosphere of the global financial crisis, revealed that merger talks between HBOS and Lloyds TSB were at an advanced stage. In the minutes before the broadcast, buyers purchased millions of HBOS shares at the deflated price of 96p; in the hour following it, they could be sold for 215p. "

It's a great example of how our faith in experts' skill, intellect or insight is so great that, for many of us, their observations and advice replace our need to assess and reflect. Put simply: they suggest it, we do it.

Of course, this brings with it real risk: surgeons, airline pilots and military leaders are amongst those who can suffer from "Captainitis" – an inflammation of the ego. In practice, this manifests itself as an unwillingness on the part of the expert to question his or her thinking, behaviour or decisions. In positions where the expert is responsible for the safety of others, there's an even greater need to challenge them but, for many people, an even greater pressure to conform, know your place in the hierarchy and respectfully obey in silence.

🔘 Try it

Who does your audience revere as an expert in the arena you're talking about? If available, use their expert insight to lend credibility to your cause just before you ask for commitment. If you can show them a quotation or some written material from an external source (website, magazine, newspaper, journal) to back this up, even better.

5. Shared Standards

Have you ever been in a situation where someone has violated something you *thought* had been previously agreed between you, or even between them and a larger group, such as an entire organization? For example, you've agreed to behave a certain way with each other, signed a contract that they've reneged on, agreed a set of company principles or values that they're behaving out of sync with. Or perhaps they're engaging in unethical or unlawful activity.

At any rate, confronting these kinds of behaviours with a, "You agreed to do *x*! You lied!" attitude is seldom useful. While we may feel vindicated using this kind of approach, we instantly create *psychological reactance*, a state of mind in the other person that causes them to put up a brick wall to our ideas. Not useful for our cause. Furthermore, these are the kind of situations that make us cringe; we like to avoid confrontation at all costs because it risks breaking social bonds and ruining our wellbeing.

In his book, *Getting More: How To Negotiate to Achieve Your Goals in the Real World* (2010), Professor Stuart Diamond of Wharton Business School outlines a priceless way of asserting yourself in such situations.[4] It involves identifying a "shared standard" that you feel has been violated. It works beautifully in two steps:

1. Putting the onus on the other person (or group) to assess their behaviour in light of that standard.
2. Asking them what they can do to remedy it if they agree that they're out of step with what was agreed.

Again, a shared standard can be a previous agreement between you and your audience, a promise, a contract, a shared value, a human principle, a law or a commonly accepted process. It's certainly not fair to use a standard that was set by you but is unknown to them, or something that they are not aware of. It needs to be commonly understood and shared.

Some useful ways to articulate step 1 are as follows:

"First name, may I ask for your thoughts on (shared standard) – how important is that to you (at work/in business/in a relationship)?"

"First name, may I ask you something: what are your personal expectations around (shared standard)?"

"First name, quick question, what standards of (shared standard) do you expect here?"

"First name, I'm confused. Didn't we agree (shared standard)?"

Step 2 is wonderful. After you have raised the issue of the shared standard, you ask them either to check their behaviour against that standard or ask them how they can behave in a way that upholds that standard, as you see fit.

Some useful ways to articulate step 2 are as follows:

"So, does what you're currently doing honour that?"

"So, how can you (achieve their outcome) in a way that upholds that standard/agreement/value?"

"So, how can we achieve (the outcome) without (behaviour that you don't want them to do)?"

The beauty of this two-step process is how respectful it is. You put the onus on them, invite them to increase their self-awareness and to create their own solutions. By doing so, you increase the likelihood that they will honour and follow through with their solutions, owing to the principles of intrinsic motivation and consistency.

 Try it

Next time someone violates a standard or agreement, do your best to stay cool. Rather than being incensed and moving into a fight or flight response, use the two-step formula:

1. Ask them for their take on the shared standard you feel has been violated.
2. Ask them how they can honour that going forward.

---

6. Demonstrate Leadership

A few years back, I enjoyed my first day of horse whispering as part of my personal and professional development. The aim of the day is to have a horse do your bidding with no physical contact: walking around you in a circle, coming in close to you when you say so, walking backwards over a log, running alongside you when you run, stopping when you stop. Pretty far out stuff.

For the first number of attempts, my horse just wasn't interested in doing my bidding. She checked me out by walking up to me and shoving me backwards fairly aggressively with her nose. I was extremely wary of horses from childhood and I must admit the experience was slightly terrifying for me.

Then the horse psychologist who was part of the team working with me disclosed an interesting thing that nowadays resides deeply in my unconscious mind. "The horse is only ever asking one question," she said, "are you the leader or not? It just wants to know if you're the one who'll protect it, keep it alive and lead it to pastures green. If you're not, it will sense it and lose interest in you."

This struck a chord with me. Isn't that true for all of us as human beings? Psychologists such as Stanley Milgram[5] and Philip Zimbardo[6] have clearly documented the need to follow authority (an alpha male or female) in their disturbing landmark studies.

So, in other words, we are deeply responsive to and influenced by those we perceive as credible experts or authority figures; those who've travelled the path before, mastered our field or have been charged with a position of power.

Once I set a clear, confident and caring leadership intention in my mind and adopted a strong, centred physiology, Seren, my horse, began to respond to my every command. When people believe that we are the credible expert, master, authority figure, guru, sage or leader in a particular field (horse pun unintended), they unconsciously give us permission to influence them and lead them.

 Try it

- Have someone your audience respects introduce you as the "leader in your field."
- Show testimonials from others explaining how you are the best bet or at least a safe one.
- Share a video, book, quotation or magazine article that shows you as the acknowledged leader or expert in your domain.
- Share a story that shows you have already walked the path they're exploring, have seen what's over the hill and can guide them safely to their destination.

The Wider Tribe: A Summary

In this chapter you may have noted that:

- We go with the majority: it affords us strength in numbers, diffuses the burden of decision making and shares the risk of embarrassment should it all go pear-shaped.
- We implicitly and explicitly agree certain norms and values within the group (aka "the done thing") that we feel uncomfortable contravening.
- We defer quickly to perceived authority within our tribes.
- We take action based on the opinions and insight that experts supply, sometimes even without thinking it through.
- Asserting ourselves is easier when we can identify a shared standard that is being violated and "hold up a mirror" to the culprit, enabling them to change.
- We seek leadership, and a leadership structure, in our tribe.

Now that you have these insights, how might you use some of these approaches to:

- Convince a difficult colleague to support your proposal?
- Challenge and alter your CEO's questionable behaviour?
- Position yourself as the front-runner for an exciting project?

In the next chapter you'll learn everyday, hypnotic techniques that'll have your audiences spinning like Catherine wheels on their insides.

CHAPTER 10
Progressive Feedback Loops

From the age of six to eight, my favourite toy was an Evel Knievel wind-up motorbike set. My older brother had the death-defying stunt bike version, while I had the easy-riding chopper. If you're of the same era, you may remember them (if not, type "Evel Knievel stunt cycle jumper 7 Inch Daredevil" into YouTube and watch!). The poseable action figure sat atop the bike, which locked into a turbo gyro – a unit with a rotating handle on the side. The faster you wound it, the more energy it built up until it took on a life of its own and raced off.

I often think about influence in that way; creating the conditions that allow your audience to move faster with more majesty and purpose to achieve amazing things. And, admittedly, sometimes people admit that I wind them up just a little.

Starting off intrinsic, positive feedback loops and growing internal states of confidence, excitement and anticipation (in ourselves and our audience) is often our job, as influencers. What follows are some examples of how you can create those united states of "Yes!"

1. Polly Wants a Cracker, Not "A Salted Biscuit"

Throughout this part of the book, we've touched on examples of how mimicking physical characteristics can produce some wonderful results. To extend this, let's look at recent research that proves, fairly conclusively, that mimicking words and phrases can also boost our power to influence generous behaviours. For fun, it's worth searching YouTube for "Bangin' Party YO!" for an example of this.

In one well-known experiment, a waitress mimics half of her diners, literally feeding back the exact words they use to order but doesn't mimic the other half of her diners. The results? Mimicry increases the number of diners who leave a tip from 52% to 78% and doubles the average tip size from 1.36 to 2.73 Dutch guilders.[1]

Come on! Surely people must be aware of being copied? Doesn't it irritate people? Or offend them, even? In the majority of studies and in practice, we see that the answer is generally that they don't when it's done subtly, so that the other person doesn't notice. However, when the mimicking is overt and seen as *inappropriate* (determined by the relationship between subject and mimicker), it can literally leave your audience feeling cold.[2] Again, it must be said that, generally, people don't realize they're being mimicked when you do it subtly because it's such a primitive, non-conscious circuit we're tapping into.[3]

What's really exciting is that a wealth of research on physical and verbal mimicry shows that it promotes pro-social behaviours beyond the people involved in the interaction, like the famous ripple effect. So, why not do it all day, every day?[4]

Try it

Wherever possible, fuse your audience's exact words and phrases into your proposition, even if they're used incorrectly or mispronounced.

2. The Power of "Yes"

My life experiences in performing arts, business, hypnosis and parenting have led me to the conclusion that we're all hardwired for "Yes!"

– that there's a natural proclivity there. I genuinely believe that it's psychologically easier to say, "Yes!" to something than it is to say, "No!" with the accompanying thoughts, challenges and expenditure of energy.

"Yes" feels good, doesn't it? When we nod or say, "Yes!" we mostly feel assured, confident, in control. So, when people around us nod slowly and regularly (known as the hypnotic nod), we tend to do the same. Watch next time you're around friends or family who are in agreement: you'll see it happening.

To back this up, researchers made the same presentation to two separate groups. Members of group two were asked to nod their heads throughout the presentation as part of an experiment. What were the take-up rates between the two groups? Group two's (the nodders) was significantly higher. Nodding says to our minds, "I'm nodding, therefore I must feel confident about this, therefore I must like this object, idea or person."[5]

The word "Yes" works in the same fashion, as do noises that convey "Yes." It's the Siamese twin of the nod. Our neurotransmitters can't help but create physical and emotional states such as certainty, excitement or determination when we repeatedly say it. The more we say it, the more certain we become of something. Attached to a nod, it's a powerful tool for others and us.

Many years ago, during my NLP (Neuro-Linguistic Programming) studies, I came across a wonderful strategy called "Yes Sets." A "set" in this context is hypno-speak for "pattern." It involves building a pattern of "Yes" responses in your audience to encourage agreement, confidence, rapport and responsiveness.

Now, versions of this have been known in business for years under various forms and names, such as "Getting them drunk of yeses," but the NLP version has a subtle difference. The traditional and slightly tacky versions take the form of asking three fast-paced closed questions that will produce "Yes" responses followed by a fourth closed question that "tricks" your audience into saying, "Yes" again through force of habit. The NLP version is more subtle and how I teach it subtler still. Ultimately, it's a fundamental approach to having two-way conversations that are focused on respect, listening, reflecting and moving towards an outcome that works for everybody. You can download the free audio programme, "D'main Authority" to learn more about this powerful approach. Just go to www.soinflow.com, click on "Free" from the navigation bar then click "Get Passcode" in the "Influence" box. After you receive and input the code, you'll find the programme in that section.

As with the traditional version, our aim is to ask questions that we know will get a "Yes" response – they don't have to say the word: a nod, "uh-huh" or an indication that they don't disagree still counts. In other words, we'll be talking about things that they cannot deny, such as *facts*, *universals* and *information they've shared with us*. If you can't confidently find something definite for them to agree with, go for something that is likely enough to provoke a "Yes" response, from what you know of them.

Two ideas can help with this first step: "universals" and "persuasive sentence openers and closers."

Universals

In NLP terminology, a "universal" is something that is true for all of us, common knowledge or widely accepted as statistically verifiable. For example, "We all like to save money for the same quality," or "We all want to be healthy," are universal truths. "It's good to have friends," is another. "Most of us like to be successful in life," another. You can even use phrases such as, "In business, time is money, wouldn't you agree?" to provoke a congruent affirmative response from your audience.

When we communicate universals to our audience, we reframe our persuasion as part of a bigger "universal" picture, sometimes referred to as "purpose." If they agree with that bigger picture, it's more likely they'll agree with a subset of it. Understanding and tapping into universals is a powerful part of a persuader's toolkit that I urge you to practise.

Persuasive sentence openers and closers

You'll instinctively know that there are some ways in which we can start and finish sentences that make it more likely we'll get the response we're after, *right?* Such as that previous sentence. Developing persuasive sentence openers and closers exponentially increases your chances of hearing "Yes" throughout your conversation. Here is a selection of common ones that people in my workshops produce and enjoy, but please develop your own that suit your style:

Openers:
- Wouldn't you agree that . . .
- Is it fair to say that . . .
- I'm guessing that . . .
- You'll know that . . .
- I take it that . . .
- I know that . . .
- Obviously . . .
- Probably . . .
- Isn't it the case that . . .
- I'm assuming that . . .
- I see you're aware that . . .
- I know that you know that . . .

Closers:
- . . . isn't it?
- . . . wouldn't you?
- . . . haven't we?
- . . . shouldn't they?
- . . . can't I?
- . . . yes?
- . . . right?

So, the Yes Set approach has two steps to it. The first step is getting a number of "Yes" responses (at least three but the more the better). The second step is converting those "Yes" responses into a new meaning for your audience and asking for commitment.

Meaning is the soul of motivation, something we search for continually in life from moment to moment. Sometimes we make useful meaning, sometimes not. The meaning we make of something determines what we do next and how we feel about it. In this technique, our job is to leverage the flood of "Yeses" to create a meaning that invites our audience to move our way.

How? Simpler than you think: by using a phrase such as, "...meaning that," "...that/which means that," or even, "...so." This redirects the affirmative information and opinion into one possible meaning. Not the only meaning but a useful and plausible one.

Here are some examples of how you can use Yes Sets, ranging from simple ways as a recap and call to action, to slightly more elegant uses:

"OK, we've seen the figures, discussed the pros and cons and highlighted our preferred choice, which means it's time to chart some actions against owners. Who can write this down?"

"Did everyone understand the scope of the challenge? Are you clear on how much funding has been cut by the latest legislation? And did I manage to convey the urgency of the situation, too? Great, so that means you must all understand the individual role you now play in that – please pledge your support financially or by volunteering via the forms that are being handed out now – even a penny or an hour of your time will help!"

"Look, I understand. You want to be treated like an adult, right? Given the same respect? Same privileges? And you know that being an adult comes with responsibilities to do certain things on time, behave a certain way, think about how other people feel and so on? Meaning that if you want the freedom to go out this weekend with your friends, you'll appreciate there are chores for you to do and agreements for us to make first? Do you get that?"

Notice that in all of these examples, the meaning posited is not necessarily *logical* but it is *plausible*.

Finally, may I make two suggestions here? The first is to keep the three "Yeses" relevant to your goal – avoid plucking random facts, universals or questions from thin air! The second is to keep your suggested commitments fairly small and sequence multiple commitments as small steps to your goal; if you make the leap too large or confusing, you'll break rapport and get a "No!"

 Try it

Use statements or ask questions that are likely to produce at least three consecutive "Yes" responses.

On receiving the three "Yes" responses, shape meaning by saying, "That/which means that . . ." "Meaning that . . ." or ". . . so," and follow on with what you would like them to think, do or choose.

For the next level iteration of this – "D'main Authority" – please visit www.soinflow.com, go to "Free," then go to "Influence" where you will find the audio programme.

Progressive Feedback Loops: A Summary

In this chapter you may have noted that:

- Repeating your audience's exact words, gestures and phrases influences them.
- Having your audience answer "Yes" repeatedly instils states of confidence, allegiance and motivation.
- Nodding creates agreement.
- Getting your audience to agree with "universal principles" or big-picture ideas drives agreement.

- Once you have multiple agreements, your suggestions about what that all means will be taken on board in a far more potent way by your audience.

Now that you have these insights, how might you use some of these approaches to:

- Placate an angry customer and show them you're on the same page?
- Reshape the meaning your loved ones are making of a difficult experience?
- Have your board realize that you need more resources for your change project?

Maybe now's an opportune time for a short summary of this part of the book. You may be pleasantly surprised at just how much you've picked up in a short space of time.

Asking with Tribes in Mind: A Summary

In this part of the book, you've looked at some very smooth relationship-building requests, hardwired through evolution. My hope is that, as you read them, you had that, "A-ha! Of course!" experience that means you already knew the approach, albeit at a nonconscious level.

You've learned how to use your body more purposefully to attract supporters, whether that's through your eyes, smile, hands, proximity, voice pitch or speed or fluency of speaking.

You've also learned how to strengthen intimate bonds with others through giving before asking, talking about obligation, flattering, asking for trust and having your trumpet blown.

You've even learned about persuading within the rules of the wider tribe through quoting the majority, using affiliation or aspiration, tapping into taboo, using insider knowledge, using other people's authority, raising shared standards and demonstrating leadership.

Finally, you've learned how to create progressive feedback loops that inspire confidence and motivation through using your audience's exact same words and phrases, nodding and building "Yes Sets."

What's next? Glad you asked. Taking the theme of "hardwired through evolution" a stage further, Part Three invites you to try out techniques that are proven to have a direct and meaningful impact on your audience's brain. In Part Three, you will learn how to become a master of the brain.

Part Three

Asking with the Brain in Mind

What's Brains Got to Do with It?

From an evolutionary perspective, we modern-day human beings in "developed" societies find ourselves in an interestingly confusing situation. Our brains have developed over tens of thousands of years to either approach or avoid certain things and experiences. Through an incredibly efficient, adaptive calibration system, we've developed brain reflexes triggered by specific stimuli, be they internal (emotional, biological) or external (social, environmental or sensory). And then, after tens of thousands of years of developing our brains to thrive in primitive environments, we go and transform the environments we live in within the space of a few hundred years to the point where they'd be almost unrecognizable to our ancestors.

The effect is that we carry a primal brain in a modern world. Our need to hunt, find shelter, have certainty and novelty, make our own choices, protect resources and status, form social groups, mate, nominate an alpha, grow, connect, trade, avoid pain, loss and social standing and be satisfied that things are fair still drive us. However, the context and environments within which we live and work have changed so dramatically that we often transfer these needs ineffectively to modern life, so that we can still meet them. I did say it was interestingly confusing.

For example, when your idea was seemingly ignored or criticized in a meeting, you may have experienced embarrassment, anger or confusion. It was your brain's emotional response system kicking in. The region of your brain called the amygdala "floods" to ready your body for invasive or evasive manoeuvres. It developed to protect you, your loved ones and your resources from life-threatening danger. Of course, situations still occur where that's appropriate, for example if you are fending off a mugger or sprinting to stop your errant two-year-old from jumping off a thirty-foot-high rock above the monkey enclosure at a Spanish zoo. Let's be honest, though: having your idea ignored isn't life-threatening but our brains still react in the same old-world way, fooling us into thinking that we're in danger.

How does this connect to making more persuasive requests, you ask? The Asks that follow tap more specifically into those primitive, hardwired aspects of our brain and psychology, to produce reflexive, non-conscious compliance.

CHAPTER 11
The Loss and Pain Brain

Arguably, we humans started from humble beginnings. Resources such as food, tools and shelter weren't easy to come by and we had to hold onto what little we had – protection and frugality would have been survival principles for our "old-world" ancestors, far more than they are for most of us today in a disposable, consumer-driven world.

So, deep-rooted in our brains is a drive to protect and be frugal. Whenever we feel we might lose some of what we have (or could have) our warning program kicks in and we experience an emotional reaction.

When Sony released its PlayStation console in 1994/1995, the world had seen nothing like it and crowds lined up outside stores buying them quicker than Sony could supply them (or perhaps *would* supply them). I remember I was working in a software sales role at that time and the prize for the company's top three producers for the month was . . . a Sony PlayStation! In a "do-anything-to-get-a-PlayStation frenzy" I triumphed as top producer that month and so qualified for the prize and, not being able to wait, I offered to drive to Toys 'R' Us myself to pick up the three consoles plus one for the CEO. I called the store to find out when they were expecting a new stock delivery and, on arriving at Toys 'R' Us that day, saw unusual numbers of people clamouring for parking spaces. A clammy wave of panic came over me. "They're all here to get PlayStations!" I said to myself, followed by an internal chant of "Gotta getta PlayStation! Gotta getta PlayStation! Gotta getta PlayStation!"

In my desperation to secure a parking place and run into the store, I took a foolish risk squeezing past a red car on my left that was reversing towards me to adjust its position. Suddenly, the black car ahead of me stopped. I stopped. The red car smashed into the side of my car, causing hundreds of pounds worth of damage. A small, angry crowd formed around me to act as witnesses for the other driver: it was my fault entirely. But that's not the punch line. As they were lecturing me and asking me for my insurance details, what was the only thing I could hear in my mind? That's right, "They're all here to get PlayStations! Gotta getta PlayStation! Gotta getta PlayStation! Gotta getta PlayStation!"

Such is the impact of losing something we have or could have. Whether it's an opportunity, a relationship, money or health, the need to avoid losing scarce resources consumes us at times, especially when mixed with a lack of certainty.[1]

It's possible that risky decisions involving potential loss use different or additional brain systems compared to risky decisions involving potential gain. In tests, people with damage to the amygdala part of their brain (necessary in decision making) can still make effective loss-based decisions but not opportunity-based decisions.[2] It runs deep. So deep, in fact, that recent brain imaging shows us that expecting a loss fires up the same brain networks as the anticipation of physical pain. The pain network, implicated in physical, social and financial pain processes, consists of the dorsal anterior cingulate cortex, insula, somatosensory cortex, thalamus and periaqueductal gray.[3]

The bottom line is this: your brain will do whatever it can to avoid losing the precious resources you've worked hard to find and may not be able to find again. The more you can do to compensate, minimize, distract or delay the brain pain your audience experiences at the point of "Yes," the more successful your requests will be.

What follows is a collection of approaches that very specifically target perceived loss and brain pain.

1. Get Charitable

At key points in the year, we in the UK gear up for three major charitable events: "Comic Relief" (aka Red Nose Day), "Children in Need" and "Sport Relief." They are times of unusual generosity, cooperation and warmth, raising over £150 million per year, placing the spotlight on worthwhile causes and bringing families, businesses and communities together.

But don't think for a moment that we do it without self-interest. Brain imaging clearly shows us that "altruism" and its associated seemingly selfless social states activate the brain's same reward circuitry as monetary or physical rewards.[4] The reward or pleasure network, implicated in physical and social rewards, consists of the ventral tegmental area, ventral striatum, ventromedial prefrontal cortex and the amygdala. The neurotransmitter called dopamine floods these areas and we feel great and motivated to do it again. The reward network, under fMRI testing, has been shown to activate equally and similarly during experiences of social, physical and monetary rewards.

What the field of neuromarketing has discovered is that, at the point of making a commitment that involves risk and brain pain,

---

Try it

- At the point of making your final request, offer a percentage of your revenues or profits to a charity – especially a charity of their choice.
- Offer to donate some of your or your organization's time as part of the deal or concession.
- Before your request, mention you've donated (on their behalf) to a cause you know they care about.

offering an opportunity to contribute to charity offsets some of the pain. If, by accepting your offer, they can do good at the same time, their brain's reward networks activate and dull the pain networks.

2. Rarities and Limited Editions

When I was a child, I used to collect and trade cards of sporting stars or superheroes – whereas younger generations collect and trade themes such as Pokémon, Dual Masters and Yu-Gi-Oh. Whatever the theme, however, there were always certain cards that few people had set eyes on, let alone possessed. Without these scarlet pimpernels, you couldn't complete your collection and so could never rest, unless you admitted defeat. In our more conspiratorial moments, we wondered whether they even existed – a sly ruse to have us all buying endless amounts of cards, perhaps. Discovering that someone in school actually had such a card carried enough potential energy to trigger a riot.

To this point, the world's most expensive baseball card sold for a hefty sum. The card was of American legend Honus Wagner; only 50 to 60 were made but what made the value soar was that only three were printed with a Piedmont cigarette ad. The fetching price? $2.8 million. Similarly, the first issue of *Action Comics* featuring Superman cost ten cents in 1938. It sold recently for $2.16 million.

Like you, the Chinese government also knows the power of scarcity. China currently exports 95% of the world's supply of rare earth metals, critical ingredients in our mobile gadgets such as phones and tablets, as well as renewable energy technology. Controversially, the Chinese government imposed serious quotas on the export of rare earth metals. The inability to import rare earth metals into the US was allegedly a key factor in Apple focusing its manufacturing operations in China, creating thousands of Chinese jobs and millions of tax dollars for the Chinese authorities. Almost like it was planned . . .

> **Try it**
>
> If you can't turn back the clock and intentionally create a limited amount of your product, service or opportunity, find a way to promote its rarity.

3. Flip the Bennies

In a study conducted at a medical clinic in the US, women were shown videos aimed at promoting HIV testing.[5]

In the control condition, information in the video was framed in terms of the benefits associated with getting tested. Only 23% of the women shown this version of the video chose to be tested within two weeks.

In the experimental condition, the information was framed in terms of the costs and risks associated with not getting tested (e.g., "By not getting tested a woman is putting herself, the people she loves and her unborn children if she becomes pregnant at risk."). Among those who saw this version, 63% chose to be tested. In similar research, loss frames have been more effective than gain frames in persuading people to obtain skin cancer detection exams[6] and in encouraging women to conduct breast self-examinations.[7]

Cialdini tells of a study in which a representative from the local power company went door-to-door offering free energy audits to homeowners. After the audit, the representative would offer products and services that could help insulate the home and lower energy costs. The representative told half of the homeowners the following: "If you insulate your home, you will save X cents per day." (The value of X was determined by the audit.) The other half of homeowners were given a slightly different pitch: "If you fail to insulate your home, you will lose X cents per day."

Critically, the information content of these two statements is identical. No incentives are being manipulated. Those who were told how much they stood to lose by not complying with the recommendation were significantly more likely to purchase the insulation. Simply flipping the coin and looking at the other side of benefits produces a tangible result. Clients of ours have increased telephone appointment books by almost 500% by using this one, simple twist.

Try it

As well as phrasing your request in terms of what your audience stands to gain or save, try phrasing it in terms of what they stand to lose should they decline (such as time, energy, money, status, opportunities). "You could save £1500 a year by choosing this," becomes, "You're currently losing £1500 a year by not doing this." "This may be a profitable opportunity for you," becomes, "Without decisive action, you may lose this opportunity."

4. Virtue and Vice

So, why is it that I nearly always eat the chocolate cake instead of the hummus?

Well, here's an experiment to explain: the next time you go shopping in the supermarket, ask yourself or your significant others, "What looks good to you?" After they have answered, ask them, "What looks good *for* you?" Are the answers the same? Typically, when I ask people this first question, they frequently answer with more tantalizing, irresistible, less healthy food items. When I ask the second question, I usually hear healthier items such as salads, fish and fruit.

The simple fact is that, for many of us, there's an interesting relationship between what we desire – *vice* – and what we know is good for us – *virtue*. Typically, many of us opt for vice as the moment of choice arises, although setting our mind on virtuous choices in the long term. Psychologists and economists often refer to this as a "present bias." Whether it's food, pastimes or even romantic partners, a temptation in the moment that has no immediate cost can lead us to take a different kind of decision. We enter what behavioural economist Dan Ariely calls a "hot state," a condition in which we choose instant gratification. Our reward circuits kick in, putting off "sensible" long-term decisions we made in a previous "cool state."

In this classic story of impulse versus constancy, a hazy uncertain future is offset by the attraction of a clear and immediate reward.

Try it

During your final request, focus on *how soon* your audience can start benefitting from using your product, service or idea and stop losing by accepting.

---

5. Buy Now, Pay Later

Recent studies show how paying with cash tilts our brain's "pain versus gain" balance more towards pain than paying with credit cards. While credit cards influence us to opt for more attractive, luxury brands, cash payments have us focus on lower-end solutions, price, delivery cost and time, installation fees and so on.[8]

An industry that uses *buy now, pay later* as standard is catalogue shopping: UK giants such as Littlewoods, Very.co.uk and Tesco all offer 12-month options for which I've been very grateful in times gone by. Retail giants Comet and Argos offer the same or similar. The brain pain is literally offset for a period of months or years on the understanding that we can pay back a small regular amount per month when the time comes. The brain thinks of the immediacy of the reward. Gain triumphs pain and the world keeps turning.

Think about taking a punch in the stomach from Mike Tyson to raise £50,000 for your favourite charity. The deal is, you can either have the normal punch and pain or you can experience no pain at the moment of impact then just 1% of the total pain each minute for 100 minutes, plus a little interest. Would you be more likely to opt for the punch with immediate pain or the punch with offset pain?

Painless being the key, it turns out that decoupling the pain of payment from the act of purchasing is a masterstroke for persuaders.

 Try it

- Give your customers a credit or credit card option. Ask them early which method of payment they'll probably opt for. During your request, focus on benefits and luxury for credit card payment; focus on practicality and cost-effectiveness for cash payments.
- If you're perceived as a luxury brand, encourage credit card payment. If your brand is mainly attractive because you're competitively priced, encourage, and even offer discounts for, paying by cash.
- Ask your family to use cash for their purchases to be more frugal.
- "Throw in" a long-term or finance option to help your audience spread the investment over a longer period of time and ease the brain pain.
- If you know and trust your audience, just let them have what you're offering and let them know they can give you the time, money or resources in the next few days, weeks or months.

6. One-Click

It was a Sunday evening a number of years ago and I was working on my Apple MacBook, preparing to travel early the next morning. I heard my then ten-year-old son asking my wife to buy him a "cheat card" for his Nintendo DS from Amazon, while she was talking to her father in Spain. Understandably, she told him, "Not now, I'm speaking to your grandfather," at which point he came to the adjoining room to make the same request of me. I told him no: I didn't have enough time right now and his mother had already told him, "No." He left.

Five minutes later, I heard him ask my wife – still on the phone – again. This time she used her "loud voice" to lightly reprimand him. He left.

Five minutes later, he appeared next to me and asked me again. I was a little irritated at his repeated undermining of his parents' authority and told him off, at which point he apologised. After a shameful, yet brief, silence, the following dialogue played out:

Son: Dad, Macs are so complicated aren't they?

Dad (suddenly experiencing major reactance): No, not at all. Far simpler.

Son: No, they're not. You have to click all sorts of things to get around, type stuff, it's really confusing.

Dad (really biting now): Not at all, that's just the way I've got mine set up – it's personalized and faster. It's just that you aren't used to it.

Son: Yeah, but for example, if Mum wants to go on the Internet on her PC, she just clicks the Internet icon.

Dad: So can I. No difference. I just prefer to do it via the keyboard.

Son: Hmmm . . . Bet Mum's computer can navigate to "Instant Replay DS" on Amazon quicker than you.

(Can you see where this is going?)

Dad (seeing where this is going but unable to resist proving that he's made good choices about his computer):   Not true! Watch! I just double tap this key, type in "Instant Replay DS" and hit that key. There, done. Loads faster than a PC.

Son (reaching over and clicking on the product image):   Wow! How cool, you're right! While you're there, press "Buy now with one-click," here's the money (places the exact cash on the table) and I'm out of your hair.

I was "gob-smacked" and realized I was at a parenting crossroads: do I reward his ingenuity, persistence and persuasiveness or do I punish his obstinacy, defiance and selfishness? I clicked the buy icon, pocketed the cash and gave him both options – a fabulous mixed message look that simultaneously said, "Not impressed but *so* impressed!"

I love buying from Amazon, as I love buying from Apple's iTunes store. Having an account set up with them, their "one-click" buying processes are so quick, simple and painless. No forms to fill out, no PayPal linking. Just click on the product you want and click to confirm you want to buy it.

Again, immediacy of reward decoupled from the pain of purchase creates a powerful incentive to go ahead with no concerns.

◉ Try it

Create a tab or account that captures your audience's transaction details legally, ethically and transparently, so they can do business with you or donate to you without the hassle of setting up any transactions or giving any more details. Aim for a one-click authorization.

7. Puppy Dog (Try before You Buy)

A friend of mine once told me a story of how, when he was little, he visited a pet shop with his parents and fell in love with a cutesy puppy dog. His parents said he couldn't have one because puppies need a lot of time, attention and energy, make a mess and so on – far too much for a little lad and busy parents to handle. Seeing his sad face, the pet shop owner pulled a masterstroke. She suggested that the only way they'd see how much was involved as a family would be to take the puppy home for a week – free of charge – and practise being owners. All they had to do was buy some dog food, toys and dog bed, leave a deposit and their contact details and she'd be happy to make it so. With nearly zero risk and a soundtrack of, "Pleeeeease? Can we? Can we?" his parents acquiesced and they took the puppy home on a trial basis.

Cut to the scene one week later, after they've all fallen in love with the little critter. It's time to take the puppy back. My friend, still a small child, is inconsolable. His parents feel their hearts being wrenched. The puppy they've named Benji has become part of their family, their routine, their life. They're used to it now. Going back, changing the new status quo, losing a friend is all too distressing. So they decide to let the pet shop owner know they'll be coming in to settle up and keep the puppy. Everyone wins.

Since writing the last paragraph, I've signed up for a 30-day free trial of Spotify's "premium" account. I've handed over my card details, so that payment will start in 30 days unless I proactively cancel. Since I'm not paying anything at this point, it was relatively brain-painless. I've used Spotify for years but now, having downloaded the fabulous Spotify iPad app and listened to music without the usual adverts, I can already see myself keeping on the subscription next month. It's likely that the pain of losing my new music listening options and flexibility will dwarf the pain of a monthly payment.

Like the "puppy dog close," the Spotify "premium" example gives us the opportunity to try something in a risk-free way, offsetting any pain involved in parting with resources, plus giving us instant gratification. All conditions the brain loves.

◉ Try it

If you're confident about the value and quality of your offering, suggest your audience takes it on a trial basis. Make sure everyone's clear about the terms and conditions of the trial before you start.

---

8. Defaults Rule

In 1985, Coca-Cola introduced "new" Coke, a move that produced such negative reactions and sales that the company had to relaunch the original cola as "Coca-Cola Classic" to pacify the public. In taste tests, ironically, pro-classic activists either couldn't tell the difference between the two, or preferred "new" Coke.

Similarly, the UK's national postal service, the Royal Mail, spent half a million pounds rebranding itself as "Consignia," a move that was so unpopular, the organization reverted to calling itself Royal Mail just one year later.

What do these examples imply? That the majority of people dislike change. It impacts their sense of certainty and triggers brain pain. We far prefer the status quo, as a rule, unless the status quo is causing us more pain than changing. This "status quo bias" is a general source of opposition to change even when people regard the consequences of the change to be a net improvement.[9]

The power of this status quo bias becomes evident when looking at international rates of organ donation. In European nations that have a system where the default is non-donation, donor rates range from roughly 4% to 27%. In European nations that presume consent as the default, and citizens have to opt out if they do not want to be donors, donor rates range from 86% to 100%. The possible explanations are that people perhaps see sticking with the status quo as:

- Recommended by experts and, therefore, a safe bet.
- A decision to go with the majority, meaning safety in numbers.
- Involving less expenditure of effort and energy than changing.
- Avoiding losing something that they currently have.

The Obama administration has several policy advisors at the vanguard of science and psychology that believe in this example of "choice architecture." Using these approaches to create national policy has certainly been a controversial tool in Obama's toolbox, dubbed "libertarian paternalism." On one hand, it guides individuals and groups to make decisions that are better for them, such as eating healthier food or saving for retirement; on the other hand, it's been criticized as "nannying" people and removing their freedom of choice. It's a controversial and highly subjective conversation.

Try it

Presume consent and set your preferred option as the default. Be transparent! Provide your audience with clear, timely details on how they can opt out, simply, if they so wish.

The Loss and Pain Brain: A Summary

In this chapter you may have noted that:

- Your ancient brain relatively suddenly finds itself in a modern world and hasn't yet fully adapted to modern-day challenges.

- The fear of losing something, especially when the way forward is unclear, generates brain pain that motivates us more than obtaining benefits and rewards.
- Including pro-social acts in your offer can offset brain pain by activating reward circuits.
- The more scarce something seems, the more your audience will value obtaining it.
- Immediacy of gratification is often important to the brain – it prefers to offset the pain and get an immediate reward.
- The brain can adjust to a new status quo quite quickly (e.g. driving a new car) but feels a sense of loss if the new status quo looks like it may be reversed.
- The brain prefers the status quo or default – it perceives it as a safer and more energy-efficient decision.

Now that you have these insights, how might you use some of these approaches to:

- Help a potential investor feel far more comfortable about injecting a large sum?
- Invite a group of customers to fall in love with your product or service?
- Secure buy-in to an optional policy change without sustained fuss?

In the next chapter you'll learn some daring, high-risk/high-reward techniques for unleashing reverse psychology, from a very visceral place.

CHAPTER 12
Reactance

Deep down, no one likes to be bossed around and dominated. Unless they're paying for it, which is a different book entirely! We all share a natural drive to protect our rights, choices and resources that we will fight for if necessary. Admittedly, it may take some of us a while to build up the courage or frustration to push back, but push back we usually will. And that will to push back is called *psychological reactance*.

If reactance is a learned response, we learn it very early on: a baby whose mother pulls away to pause while breastfeeding will demonstrate it at volume. The key bit of grey matter kit that's involved here is our amygdala, an almond-shaped mass of nuclei located deep within the temporal lobe of the brain. It's an age-old bit of the limbic system that is deeply connected to the processing and memory of emotion. When you feel that a personal boundary has been crossed (safety, status, freedom, intimacy and so forth), it triggers an adrenaline response that initiates either "fight or flight" behaviours or sometimes "tend and befriend."

Reactance is a very powerful form of motivation, which carries tremendous energy with it. Harry Enfield's character, Kevin the teenager, is a tremendous example of living with a reactant. Very often, reactance isn't pretty but if you can tap into and piggyback this energy, your audience will carry your cause with unstoppable momentum.

So there I am, aged 17, wanting to drive 30 miles into the local city to see a band with my mates. But none of my friends who have passed their driving test can borrow their parents' cars that evening. And, as I have not passed my test yet, I can't drive without a qualified driver sitting alongside.

Now, I don't know why, but what I actually said was, "There is no way you would want me to drive in with one of my mates in charge." And guess what, he said it was okay. I was surprised but afterwards I looked back and realized I had stumbled on a very effective way of getting straight to yes. A way that I have used many times since.

The technique is to acknowledge the other person's biggest fear and agree that because of this we shouldn't take the action, despite its obvious benefits. First, the other person hears that you understand their worries. Second, it seems to me that many of us automatically see counterarguments and problems with what others say. So, by framing our request as "we couldn't" most people seem to respond by arguing how we could.

Thankfully, the car came back without a scratch and I learnt an important lesson in getting straight to yes.

By Clive Hutchinson, Owner, Cougar Automation Limited www.cougar-automation.com

1. The "Take-Away"

Years ago, in a very aggressive sales industry, we were told to use the lines, "It *is* luxurious. It's *not* for everyone," early during our sales pitch. Furthermore, if we had a potential customer who consistently objected to our product but displayed (or whose partner displayed) a glimmer of interest, we were taught to start packing up our materials, literally *taking away* the deal from the table while adding, "Sorry, I hope I haven't wasted your time, I just don't think this is for you, do you?" High risk? Admittedly. Confrontational? Intentionally.

Frequently, though, it would create such a strong "forbidden fruit" reflex in our prospects that they (typically the men) would reach across the table and physically stop us from putting our materials away. They would then tell us (and themselves, more importantly) exactly why it was for them, specifically how they could use it and precisely how they could afford it, whatever it cost. Deal done.

What was at play was another version of loss, provoked by what psychologists call reactance.[1] Reactance is the attitude we develop as children and especially as teenagers to protect our autonomy and assert our independence. If you have teenagers, you'll see this daily: if you say, "Do," they say, "Don't." If you say, "Black," they say, "White." Reactance kicks in when people tell us what to do or even suggest something to us: we're hardwired to prefer a homegrown solution rather than an imported one, to prefer buying rather than being sold to and to prefer learning rather than training.

Try it

When you know your audience is interested but they're acting in a consistently objectionable way, figuratively or even literally "take away" the offer to trigger reactance.

2. Polar Asking

Once he hit puberty, my dear older brother became perhaps the most contrary person I know. If I said a band was great, he'd quote reviews that categorically proved otherwise. His main counterargument sentence openers, "Technically . . ." and "I think you'll find . . ." became so frequent that, ultimately, they became a source of great entertainment to me and my friends.

I remember with relish the day I said the opposite of what I believed and had him disagree with it, thus agreeing with my true intention. This then developed into my magical phrase, "I know you'll disagree with me but . . ." which, again, had him disagree with the fact that he would disagree with me, thus agreeing with me!

Such behaviour is called "mismatching" and is an extremely strong reactance reflex. The "mismatcher" continually perceives their value or their options as being restricted or neglected in some way and, naturally, pushes to reassert. This, by the way, often explains how certain people can inexplicably disagree with your most inert suggestion: often they're restating boundaries they feel have been infringed either by the style of the interaction – *how, where, when* or *why* you're asking them – or by a previous interaction that they disliked and are now paying you back for.

I was once presenting to a panel of directors, offering my company's services and while all were enjoying the interaction, one in particular kept disagreeing with most of what I was saying, to the point of distraction. I ended up saying, "I think I know your thinking 100%, (difficult director). You know that it's worth going back to the drawing board and taking a few more months to do some extra focus groups and engaging with a few more suppliers over the next few months. Isn't that right?" He recoiled in disgust and stated that my inference was not true at all, that speed was of the essence and we should just get started with my company immediately without extra fuss or diagnostic work. With someone who has a track record of opposition to your direct requests, intentionally tapping into this mismatching behaviour by stating the opposite of what you want is a high risk but often wildly effective persuasive ploy.

 Try it

With mismatchers, try suggesting that they'll disagree with your suggestion before you make it.

3. Forbidden Fruit and Response Potential

Years ago, I remember a particularly annoying colleague of mine waving a box of pizza in front of another colleague who was on a diet with an accompanying sonic taunt of "Mmmmmm!" The intimation was, "I can have this and you can't." Very mature. What was equally mature was my dieting colleague snatching a slice and eating it with an accompanying, "Mmmm!" after the owner momentarily glanced away. People hate being told what they can't do, can't be or can't have: it triggers instant reactance.

Repeated over time, this can become a highly potent force that we can use to our advantage. For example, when my children were small, I used to voice such classic lines as, "No, you can't have them – Brussels sprouts are only for grown ups," every time we would have Brussels sprouts. Not that they wanted them in any way but consistently reclassifying Brussels sprouts as forbidden fruit eventually resulted in them asking, nay, demanding to have sprouts on their plates. "That's easy," you say, "what about when they eat them and they taste awful?" Well, the weird thing is that because they have attached such importance to obtaining the forbidden fruit, they convince themselves that they enjoy their spoils, while pulling a face like they've just eaten a whole lemon. As the Marquis de Sade was famous for saying, "Some of our greatest pleasures are derived from conquered repugnances." The truth is, they savour the process (the anticipation, effort and achievement), not the prize.

The technique is known as building response potential: continually saying "No" to create reactance, until they're more eager than a beaver in "Twigs 'R' Us." You can even use this to create desire and motivation where there was none before – your audience's reactance to having their options curtailed will take care of that.

Whether you want to create a feverish "kid on Christmas Eve" state in your audience so they demand to take on a particular responsibility, use a particular venue or be included in a preferred customer or supplier list, building response potential is a great tool to pull out.

 Try it

Find a way to explicitly label your outcome as "off limits for *you*" or "something they're not quite ready or qualified for yet" to create an intensifying effect on your audience's desire.

Reactance: A Summary

In this chapter you may have noted that:

- Reactance is a deep response to our rights, choices or resources coming under perceived threat.
- Reactance affects the amygdala area of the brain as well as other areas and initiates a "fight or flight" response in some people; a "tend and befriend" response in others.
- Saying, "It's not for everyone," can trigger mild reactance.
- When your audience is even vaguely interested, taking away a product, service or option can trigger reactance and a greater desire to obtain it.

- Certain people, "mismatchers," experience reactance constantly, with small things; saying "I'm sure you'll disagree with me but . . ." before your point, usually makes them agree with you.
- Suggesting something is a forbidden fruit causes reactance and a greater desire to obtain it.

Now that you have these insights, how might you use some of these approaches to:

- Transform your sales offer into a "must-have" in the space of a few seconds?
- Entrap an admin clerk into agreeing with you wholeheartedly?
- Have your children treat something as a privilege?

In the next chapter you'll tap deep into the matrix in which we're sleepwalking to add some persuasion code or wake up your audience.

CHAPTER 13
Pattern Breakers

Have you ever been driving your car or travelling a familiar route on public transport and had that moment where you suddenly "wake up" and think to yourself, "How on earth did I get here? I must have zoned out!" As mentioned previously, the non-conscious parts of our brain take charge of repetitive tasks, such as breathing, regulating body temperature and – sometimes – driving. It frees brainpower for us to use in more complicated information processing and decision-making tasks that typically involve the most recently evolved part of our brain, known as the pre-frontal cortex (PFC).

Essentially, we're on autopilot most of the time, even though we'd like to think we're exerting conscious control over events. This means that, most of the time, your audience is on autopilot, too. The approaches that follow are ones that tap into, or break, that bubble of trance.

1. The Pique Technique

"Hello, sir, my name is Marley, from ABC Ltd, do you have a spare minute to help us with a survey?"

What would be your reflex response if propositioned with such a request while going about your business? Typically, most of us say something like, "Err, no, sorry, I haven't time today," knowing that 60 seconds in our schedule isn't, in fact, going to break the bank. So, why do we respond in such a way? Probably to help us avoid getting into situations where we'll make commitments of time, money or energy; far better to nip it in the bud with a pre-prepared, hardwired response psychologists call a "refusal script."

So how did researchers increase the frequency of donations from passersby from 18.8% to a high of 87.1% while increasing donations from ¢7 to ¢38 in the process? By using the concept of "piquing."

In 1994, researchers ran a field study.[1] In the control condition, the experimenter said, "Excuse me, can you spare a quarter/any change?" whereas in the pique condition the line was, "Excuse me, can you spare ¢17 (or ¢37?)." In the pique condition, compliance increased by almost 60%.

When we pique someone's curiosity, we interrupt what he or she expects to hear with something novel, arousing his or her mind. Essentially, we bypass the pattern that runs the refusal script because they have no pre-prepared response for our novel behaviours or requests.

Try it

When you are making a request, use atypical prices (£1095.16; a penny less a pound), amounts (327 units; enough to fill a jumbo jet), conditions (we'll deliver it with a cheeky grin; we'll ask for a "trust" payment upfront of $n) or times (available for the next 17-and-a-half minutes; meet at 4:18pm precisely) to pique your audience's curiosity and bypass their refusal scripts.

2. Disrupt then Reframe (DTR)

A creative extension of the pique is the disrupt-then-reframe technique. It involves breaking your audience's autopilot pattern with a pique that you subsequently resolve through a reframing suggestion.

In Eric Knowles's experiments, he sold packs of Christmas cards to participants for $3 with a rough sales ratio of 40%. However, the sales ratio jumped to 80% when he explained to participants, "The price of eight cards is 300 pennies, which is a bargain." By piquing their curiosity with, "300 pennies," an atypical way of saying three dollars, and then reframing this as, "a bargain," Knowles boosted his success considerably.[2]

For example:

"Could you lend me half of 100 dollars, please? It's just a super-safe, 24-hour loan."

"Each one gives you five pennies change from a fiver; that's an unbeatable price!"

"We're asking you to volunteer a single waking hour every 30 days, which is a small, yet generous way of helping."

 Try it

Find a creative way to describe elements of your request in an atypical way, then reframe it with an accompanying suggestion.

---

3. Just Because . . .

In 1978, psychologists Langer, Blank and Chanowitz conducted an interesting experiment on mindfulness.[3] It is widely interpreted as evidence that giving a reason after making a request increases the compliance rate dramatically.

The psychologists had experimenters attempt to "queue jump" or "cut the line" at a photocopier. Request one was, "Excuse me, I have 20 pages. May I use the Xerox machine?" This produced a 60% compliance rate. Request two was, "Excuse me, I have 20 pages. May I use the Xerox machine, because I'm in a rush?" which produced a 94% compliance rate. Request three was, "Excuse me, I have 20 pages. May I use the Xerox machine, because I have to make copies?" Although this third request may seem absurd, because that's what everyone was waiting for, this resulted in a 93% compliance rate.

The bigger the request got, the less likely an absurd reason sufficed for compliance, but giving a reason improved the compliance rate each time. The magic word in this? "Because." Exasperated parents know the power of because after being asked, "Why?" for the 6,000th time, often responding: "Oh . . . just because! All right?"

Try it

Give a reason with your request, ". . . because I'm hungry" or ". . . because it would be great for business" or ". . . because it would mean the world to me," because, statistically, it will make your request more effective.

---

4. Dump and Chase (DAC)

Perhaps, the most difficult obstacle to overcome when persuading is when your audience presents no obstacle at all. Rather, they offer a flat "No" with zero explanation, even when you enquire. When our audience does voice an obstacle (an objection or concern), at least we have a chance to help them remove it or move around it. It's the absence of the chance to address any obstacle that makes a flat "No" such a passion killer.

Unsurprisingly, in one study, this child-like (read as "socially uninhibited") approach of asking, "Why not?" followed by an attempt to remove or reframe the obstacle was found to be the silver bullet of all persuasion plays.[4] For example:

Asker: "Mayra, I need to take care of some business in the library there and I forgot the lock for my bike. It should take about ten minutes. Will you watch my bike for me until I return?"

Asked: "Sorry, I can't."

Asker: "Why not?"

Asked: "Erm, well, I'm . . . supposed to be preparing for a meeting this afternoon."

Asker: "What do you need to prepare?"

Asked: "Just a pad and pen, I suppose."

Asker: "Cool. Here's a pad and pen, keep them. You could prep now while I take care of business in the library. Could that work?"

Asked: "Uh, well, yes, I suppose. OK, that's fine."

◎ Try it

Make a direct request of your audience. If they refuse, ask, "Why not?" and remove or reframe the obstacle. We're not always clear on why we refuse in the moment – sometimes it's just a gut feeling – so be prepared to repeat the process two or three times before they articulate the real obstacle.

The DAC does, however, rely on you coming up with a great reframe or objection-handling response, so if you're not yet agile in this area, it may be one to practise in low-risk settings before relying on it in the field.

5. An Honest Reflection

Why do so many shops have circular mirrors attached to the ceiling or CCTV cameras that feature you as the star of the screen? Surely, if it was just for identifying criminals to the authorities, they'd be discreetly tucked away, to avoid spoiling the ambience? And don't you suddenly feel more self-conscious when you see yourself in a mirror or on screen?

It turns out that seeing ourselves in some form induces honest behaviour. It's another autopilot interruption: to our distant ancestors, seeing themselves was certainly not a normal occurrence. To validate this, Arthur Beaman and his team executed some very creative research in the late '70s.[5]

Eighteen houses were studied in trick-or-treat scenarios one Halloween. In total, 363 children were instructed by the house owner to take one sweet. The owner then left the kids to their own devices. 33.7% of children took more than one sweet. However, in houses where a mirror was positioned so that children would see themselves taking the sweet, the amount that took more than one sweet dropped to 3.9%. In the second experiment, where no adult appeared to communicate any kind of limit or expectation, children who saw themselves in the mirror still took fewer sweets.

Perhaps the phrase, "How can she even look at herself in the mirror?" when referring to perceived dishonest behaviour is yet another example of our language carrying the source code of influence.

 Try it

When making requests where you wish your audience to act honestly or pro-socially, see if you can ask them next to a mirror in which they can see their reflection.

---

6. Caught on Camera

Peace One Day founder, Jeremy Gilley, carried out a version of this technique to extraordinary effect. Gilley had a simple, yet epic mission of bringing about world peace, starting with a single day of peace, designated and ratified by the United Nations. Talk about ambitious. To do this, he enlisted politicians, pop stars, actors and activists around the world to help him in his endeavour.

Gilley is, by trade, a filmmaker. Arguably, the masterstroke in the early days of his campaign was the decision to make a documentary of his quest, meaning that all his meetings were explicitly filmed. Put another way, every politician or actor he met was made aware that the conversations were being filmed for a documentary on peace, which large numbers of people would see. As Gilley says, who could refuse to be filmed for a documentary about bringing peace to the world? If they did refuse, it would be mentioned on the documentary and surely would be a slight on the world's perception of them. If they complied, their behaviour, attitudes and commitments would go on record, holding them accountable in public.

Perhaps it was inevitable, then, that Gilley managed to persuade the UN and associated NGOs to make 21st September every year "World Peace Day." Even the Taliban agreed to put down their weapons on that day, so that supplies and medicine could flow freely to those who needed it most.

As a result of the campaign, more than a million children are now immunized against polio each year by WHO and UNICEF, as well as a host of other incredible commitments to peace, in one of the most war-torn, economically deprived areas in the world. If Gilley can persuade people to do that, what excuse do we have in persuading our bosses to give us a pay rise?

 Try it

Find a way to create an honesty-inducing fly-on-the-wall video project that holds your audience accountable on camera.

Pattern Breakers: A Summary

In this chapter you may have noted that:

* Asking for something unusual or asking for what you want in unusual ways often bypasses pre-prepared defence mechanisms.
* Presenting the benefits of your offering after phrasing something in an atypical way has the perceived effect of amplifying those benefits.
* Reasons rock and we're more successful when we use them with every request.
* Asking "Why not?" after a "No" is ultra powerful when we can provide a strong counter-argument.
* Seeing our reflection or being aware that we are being monitored causes us to behave more honestly and to uphold higher moral standards.

Now that you have these insights, how might you use some of these approaches to:

- Jump a queue at the airport if you're worried about missing your flight?
- Get your desired concession after a flat "No" response at the negotiating table?
- Grab your most desired contact's time and attention at a conference?

In the next chapter you'll learn some highly unusual, yet subtle cue-based approaches that don't even need you to say anything to work their mojo.

CHAPTER 14
Priming

There's a terrific episode of Derren Brown's TV series *Mind Control*[1] in which he instructs a design agency to design a poster for a chain of taxidermy stores, including a new company name, a strap line and a logo. It's all their choice. Ostensibly. Ultimately, they produce exactly the same name, logo and strapline that Derren has pre-prepared, sketched out and sealed in an envelope *before the process started*. It's frightening and worth watching. And sorry for spoiling the ending.

In his recent masterpiece, *Thinking Fast and Slow*, Nobel prize winner Daniel Kahneman outlines our two systems of thinking. "System 1" thinking is intuition: ancient, fast and non-conscious, influenced by knowledge, beliefs and emotion; "system 2" thinking is reasoning: unique to humans, evolutionarily recent, slower, deliberate, more conscious.

Kahneman describes how we're wrong to associate mostly with system 2 – in fact, system 1 rules us most of the time. System 2 tires easily (called "ego depletion") and hands over to the wisdom of its older, wiser sibling. But because system 1 works so quickly and has evolved from a different age, it has certain issues. First, it's unbelievably biased: it thinks that all it can see is all there is and only pays attention to what it knows. Second, it takes in vast amounts of information, is influenced by that information, makes a decision and lets system 2 know what the decision is. But it neglects to tell system 2 its reasoning; that's for system 2 to guess.

That's what happens in the Derren Brown episode: deliberately placed non-conscious cues on their journey to work, such as flyers, landmarks and names all lead the designers to create what the mentalist extraordinaire wants them to create.

Our environment influences in ways that we're only just starting to appreciate, and it's a lot greater an influence than you might expect.

Using our surroundings to influence our results is a nice idea but what if you haven't the time, energy or resources to make that happen? Research into the influence that tactile sensations have on our judgement is a fascinating area of study. The kinds of object that we touch and the physical properties of those objects, such as texture, temperature and weight, have a meaningful impact on our subsequent decisions.

What follows is a bevy of examples detailing how you can use your environment to aid your outcome, along with some simpler, more spontaneous and mobile ideas to play with.

1. A Brief Case of Priming

If you've ever spent time in Microsoft's UK headquarters, you might come out raving about the environment: casual dress, a lake with wild ducks and a summerhouse packed with free refreshments, mini golf, multiple restaurants, foosball tables, X-boxes, colours, comfy sofas and so on, all of which employees and suppliers use daily as their meeting or private working environment. It's a purposeful design to influence the kind of culture the company wants, as is the decision to create an open-plan office for open communication, or a closed-plan office for privacy. Intentionally or otherwise, we shape our environment and it shapes us right back.

For example, did you hear that higher ceilings foster greater creative thinking?[2] As does seeing the Apple logo.[3] Or that messy environments subconsciously prime us to simplify our choices and pay more for that simplicity, especially, if you're politically conservative.[4]

Extending this phenomenon, anthropologists tell us that material objects are loaded with meaning, as to cultural norms and values, in any given society's collective consciousness. For example, soft lighting and candles instantly suggest . . . romance. All white decor with a minimalist use of furniture suggests . . . a Zen meditative function (or that your mortgage is massive and you can't afford anything else). Purple and gold decor is often used in hotels to connote opulence and luxury. And one study showed how angry students become measurably more aggressive after casual exposure to a gun.

Many years ago, a company sales trainer advised me to carry an ultra-slim briefcase into important client meetings with only one document – the contract – inside. Why? The bigger the briefcase, the fuller and more sprawling its contents; the fuller the contents, the lower the value of each page; the lower the value of each page, the lower the value of the owner. She was right. Instead, I opted for a soft messenger bag with a shoulder strap. Call me a fashionista.

In Stanford, Kay and Ross ran a test where one group was exposed to objects associated with business, such as boardroom tables and briefcases, while another group saw neutral objects such as kites and toothbrushes. Immediately after, groups were set tasks surreptitiously measuring how cooperative or competitive each was thinking and behaving. Consistently, groups "primed" with business objects demonstrated more competitive behaviour but denied that exposure to business-related objects had influenced their behaviour in any way.

Especially when we're unclear what's expected of us, we look to external cues to guide our behaviour. As the experimenters said, "We're simply not conscious of how many of the things all around us affect our behaviour."[5]

2. Escalate Your Thinking

It's a strange phenomenon that our everyday language often holds deep scientific truth. We speak about feeling "uplifted" as a positive. People talk about "getting high" as something far out. We "step up,"

> ## Try it
>
> - When you want people to choose the simple option, ask them in a messy environment.
> - If you want to encourage competition, adorn your environment with objects or images associated with business. For cooperative behaviours, feature objects and images associated with sharing and teamwork. For an informal culture, feature objects and images associated with social situations. For creativity, choose high ceilings or use Apple products.

"raise our game" and "rise to the challenge." Of course, we sometimes talk about feeling "low," "down" or "depressed" as conditions we'd rather avoid.

No surprise, then, that Larry Sanna's brilliant experiments on pro-social behaviour produced the intriguing conclusion that elevating our vertical height produces more pro-social actions.

There were four studies published. In the first study, shoppers travelling up the escalators gave to charity 16% of the time versus downward travellers' 7% and regular shoppers' 11%. In the second and third studies, participants sitting higher up (versus lower down) helped another person longer and acted with more compassion. In the final study, watching a video of scenes shown from a higher perspective led to a 60% increase in pro-social behaviour.[6]

Could it be that the closer people get to the heavens, the more godly and benevolent their behaviour? Could it also explain why, in certain cultures, man traditionally proposes on one knee to his beloved? In other words, artificially creating an "elevated state" in his intended? It's worth remembering that evolution is not just about survival of the fittest from a genetic standpoint: "survival of the fittest" also applies to ideas (known as "memes").

Anything that can increase social cohesion is rewarded in our brain and body with "feel good" hormones and neurotransmitters such as oxytocin, serotonin and endorphins. It's Nature's way of saying, "Yes, that's it! Do more of that!" to encourage us to stay alive, stay in tribes and procreate successfully.

Try it

- So, people act more generously when uplifted, it seems. If you're asking for assistance, donations or any kind of altruistic commitment, it would make sense to locate your request station at the top of escalators, steps, stairwells, buildings or other elevated settings.
- This approach is a one-off – not to be overused with any one individual. When you need to make a really big Ask of someone you know well, consider getting down on one knee, with a broad smile and a light heart, to make your request. To further amplify the effect, do it when others are around.

---

3. Hot Coffee, Harvey?

Recent brain scans have shown the brain's insular cortex to be involved in processing information pertaining not only to experiences of physical warmth, but of psychological, interpersonal warmth. Often, we call this psychological feeling of warmth "trust" and it's arguably the single most important and desirable personality trait of all. When we are rejected (see "The outstretched hand" in Chapter 7), the insular cortex becomes highly active, with interesting results.

When researchers experimented to see whether experiencing physical and psychological warmth were one and the same, they were amazed. Test subjects who briefly held a cup of hot coffee judged a target person as having a warmer, more caring and generous personality, compared to those who briefly held some iced coffee. Similarly, test subjects who held a hot therapeutic pad more frequently chose a gift for a friend instead of for themselves, compared to the cold holders.[7]

While we're on the subject of coffee… Studies from 2005 showed that caffeine makes us easier to persuade, as well as boosting memory recall. Students in support of euthanasia were given an orange juice drink, with half of the group's juice secretly containing two espressos' worth of caffeine. Having read counterarguments to euthanasia, the newly caffeinated students appeared to have softened their attitudes measurably more so than the students who drank normal orange juice.[8]

Try it

- Before meeting someone, rub your hands together vigorously, to create the friction that will warm up your hands. Alternatively, wear woollen gloves, place them under a hand dryer or keep a gel heat pack in your pocket. Never shake hands with cold hands if you can help it.
- Always offer your audience a cup of coffee or other hot drink at the beginning of meetings. And have one yourself.

4. Mass Influence

Recently, I came across some research that shed light on why I always feel slightly let down when I get a feather-light paper menu when sitting down to dinner in a classy restaurant. To me, it just feels wrong.

Holding a heavy clipboard influenced male passersby, but not females, to allocate more money to social issues compared to when holding a light clipboard. A heavy clipboard also led both genders to rate an attached resumé as better and more serious about the job, than when attached to a light clipboard. The weight of the clipboard did not affect, however, perceptions of how likely the owner of the resumé was to get along with others. Interestingly, those who held a heavy clipboard rated the importance of their accuracy on the task more highly than light clipboard holders but didn't report putting any extra effort into it.[9]

In other studies, the perceived quality, expected price and liking ratings of food and wine increased as the weight of the dish[10] or bottle[11] increased. Increasing the mass of a seemingly irrelevant object can strengthen the "gravity" of our experiences. Which is why I always feel let down with a light menu in a classy restaurant: my perception of the value is influenced by the weight of the menu. As is, perhaps, the enjoyment of the experience, tip, referrals and repeat visits.

Try it

- Print out your proposal, report, price list or menu on thicker paper and attach it to a heavy backing such as a high-quality clipboard or menu holder. Or hole-punch it and place it in a heavy folder.
- Give your audience something heavy to hold, like a paperweight, when you want them to interpret your request as more important.

---

5. Comfy Chair

How do the chairs in your organization's boardroom or meeting rooms compare to the seating in your local coffee shop or your living room? Are the boardroom seats warmer, softer, more giving and accommodating or are they firmer, more rigid and more independent? Do you think you'd feel more playful sitting on a beanbag or an executive chair?

.

The earlier-mentioned fascinating study by Bargh *et al.* had people sitting on either a hard, wooden chair or a soft, cushioned chair, making an offer on a car. When their first offer was rejected, test subjects sitting on the soft chairs were far more likely to make a bigger change in their offer price compared with the hard chair subjects. As the researchers concluded, "Thus, hardness produces perceptions of strictness, rigidity, and stability, reducing change from one's initial decisions, even when the touch experience is passive in nature."[9]

 Try it

If you want more flexibility from your audience, sit them on soft seating or ask them in an informal setting with sofas, such as a café. If you need to stick to your guns, sit yourself in a hard chair.

6. Teenage Tidiers

When my wife was 16 years old, I remember being unable to walk from one side of her bedroom to the other without standing on a book, record, chocolate wrapper or item of clothing. It's a well-worn cliché that teenagers' attitudes to orderliness can be, let's say, *challenging* for their parents. So, could one of the greatest, most useful Asks of all time be the one that has them agree to tidy up?

Well, apparently, the scent of lemons makes us tidy more. In the fabulously titled study, "Smells like clean spirit," students eating in a lemon-scented room (courtesy of citrus-scented cleaning liquid in a large bucket of warm water) cleaned up their crumbs approximately three and a half times more than those in an unscented room.[12]

> ### Try it
>
> - Before you ask your teenager to tidy up, put a healthy amount of citrus-scented cleaner in a bucket of warm water outside their door.
> - Place a citrus-scented air freshener in your teenager's room, so they adopt tidier behaviours.

7. Possession is 9/10 of the Sale

Many years ago, I sold real estate overseas. The high point of the presentation was taking them to our newly built five-star apartment complex and, specifically, to the showrooms where we would encourage them to touch things to feel the quality, sit on the sofa, change the channel on the TV, try out the stereo and even lie on the bed (we stopped short of asking them to try out the bath or the toilet).

The reason we did this was to make the experience real to them, to get them to "try it on," imagine owning it and connect them to the property, rather than having a purely abstract, rational, emotionally disconnected relationship with it.

In many markets around the world, market traders offer free samples to create obligation and encourage reciprocity, but in the vibrant open markets where I lived at the time, they'd take it a step further to encourage ownership. The most successful fruit sellers would actually throw delicious pieces of fruit to passersby, shouting, "Catch!" As soon as a passerby caught a piece of fruit, they'd eat it, more often than not. More often than not, they'd enjoy it and engage the seller to buy more.

Similarly, a former boss of mine taught me a very playful way of popping the contract-signing question. He instructed me to have the client look through the contract and, once their questions were answered, to say, "Over to you," and, with a ludic smile on my face, roll a good-quality, heavy, uncapped pen across the table to them. As the pen reached the end of the table and dropped off, their reflex would be to catch the pen. With readied pen in hand, they'd be more likely to take action and sign the contract, rather than deliberating further. I thought it cheesy and didn't try it until, years later, it accidentally just happened with a client and worked like a charm. Not only that, but the client raved for months about the playfulness, boldness and style of my request. Very occasionally, I find myself using it but only when there is a shared sense of humour between myself and the other party.

Unsurprisingly, recent scientific studies support these practices. In 2009, Joann Peck and Suzanne Shu ran experiments on the perceived effects of touch and ownership.[13] In four studies, they found that touching an object increases the feelings of ownership a person has for the object, compared to not touching it. They also showed that these touch-induced feelings lead to higher price valuations of the object, compared to not touching it. On average, the valuation was $3.59 in the touch condition and $3.34 in the no-touch condition – a 7% shift. Imagine a 7% shift in your revenues.

What's also interesting is that they found that when it's not possible to touch your product (for example, if you're offering it online or if you're offering a service) "consumers respond effectively to the combination of no touch and ownership imagery." In other words, showing images of people using your product or service taps into our mirror neurons, causing a "monkey see, monkey do" experience.

Brilliantly, Peck and Shu quote from the film *Star Trek: First Contact*[14] to communicate their findings:

Captain Jean-Luc Picard: It's a boyhood fantasy . . . I must have seen this ship hundreds of times in the Smithsonian but I was never able to touch it.
Lieutenant Commander Data: Sir, does tactile contact alter your perception?

Captain Jean-Luc Picard: Oh Yes! For humans, touch can connect you to an object in a very personal way.

Try it

Wherever and whenever possible, invite your audience to touch, handle, caress or examine your offering. If it's not possible, present them with ownership imagery. If your only tool is words, ask them to imagine themselves using or owning it and ask them questions to elaborate on the ownership experience.

Priming: A Summary

In this chapter you may have noted that:

- Our non-conscious mind processes and is influenced by vast amounts of environmental cues, stimuli and information completely outside of our awareness. It then makes decisions for us without telling us how it came to that conclusion and our "conscious" mind fools itself into thinking it's in control.
- Objects in our environment are metaphors, full of cultural associations, which can direct our non-conscious mind and behaviour intentionally or unintentionally.
- The temperature, texture or weight of things we touch with our bodies will influence how we contextualize what is going on around us and inside us.
- Touching makes us more desirous of owning or thinking we already do.
- Always have warm hands before shaking hands and give your audience a hot drink immediately.
- Create soft, informal seating or surroundings for more flexible, open interactions.

- Use heavy paper, bottles, pens or clipboards to signify importance and value.

Now that you have these insights, how might you use some of these approaches to:

- Secure more contributions of time and money for your cause?
- Increase your customer's perceived ownership of your products?
- Influence your colleagues to think more flexibly about a difficult issue?

Shall we briefly review this part of the book? See how much is familiar from this part and previous parts – it all hangs together, you know . . .

Asking with the Brain in Mind: A Summary

In this part of the book, you've delved deep into the structures of the brain to make sense of how our persuasion attempts can create very real effects on a neurological level. You've looked at how the brain's primary focus on *approach* or *avoidance* behaviours means we're constantly calculating risk and certainty. How your audience's brain generates pain through the same networks used for physical pain when there's a risk of losing stuff. And how to tap into that.

You've learned that most of us create reactance – push back – for the tiniest perceived infringements of our boundaries, such as status, comfort, autonomy, resources or rights. Even a phrase such as someone saying, "If I were you, I'd do . . ." triggers reactance and you learned how to reverse this play to profit, as well as labelling what you're offering as *forbidden fruit*.

Frighteningly, you've read about how, most of the time, we're on non-conscious autopilot, ruled by system 1 thinking as a way to be quicker and more efficient. You've probably picked up a few new approaches to leverage this or snap your audience out of their trance to promote different behaviours.

Finally, you're now clued up on how our environment can shape our thoughts – everyday cues that prime us to think or behave in specific ways such as temperature, weight, height, physical touch or smell – and how you can use that to stack the odds in your favour.

What's next? At this point of the journey, we've covered all of the approaches I wanted to share with you. So, what follows is a short final section to contextualize what you have been gathering, throwing in some important *dos* and *don'ts* about making your persuasion stick. And helping you come up with a plan of action to turbocharge your fortunes.

Part Four

Commencement

CHAPTER 15
Actively Reflect

Where Are You Now?

Welcome to an exclusive minority! Other than our clients and the forward-thinking individuals who've bought this book, there are few people I'm aware of with access to such a solid, trailblazing repertoire of influence techniques. As you start to think where, when and how you'll employ this new learning, I'd like to offer you a few questions to reflect on, to get the most out of your learning experience. You might consider writing the answers down in a journal, having a con versation with a friend or colleague or something else entirely. Take your time with them.

- How do I feel now about my emerging capabilities? Tingling? Responsible? Guilty? Powerful? Something else entirely?
- What was familiar to me?
- What was new or different to me?
- Did any of the techniques cross a boundary for me? If so, which techniques and boundaries?
- Which stories or examples can I bring to mind that particularly resonated with me?
- In what ways do I now recognize having been on the *receiving* end of certain techniques, whether as a customer, colleague or supplier?

- What do I believe about asking that's empowering and new?
- What are the positive things I'm realizing are most important to me when it comes to asking?
- In the context of making persuasive requests, how would I complete the sentences, "From now on, when it comes to getting straight to 'Yes,' I am . . ." and "I now realize that getting straight to 'Yes' is . . ."

Readiness

I'm sure you understand that it's fine if not every technique or every part of the book lit you up like a Christmas tree! My hope is that if you can take *even one approach* that you adopt and find success through, you'll have a return on your investment many times over.

Frankly, at this stage, I want you to get on and start making a difference to yourself and those you serve, so I'll aim to keep this final part of the book brief. You've covered a fair bit of material; you may even have experimented with certain techniques as you read through. Some may have worked, others not, first time around. It's a funny old world sometimes. With a chunky collection of material such as this, it's a good idea to identify your favourites, whittle them down to two or three and then prepare, experiment and refine in a low-risk scenario until you get to grips with them. As you find approaches you love, feel comfortable with and find success with, you can build your collection. Doing too much, too soon isn't big and isn't clever.

Fine-Tuning

Becoming someone to whom people enjoying saying, "Yes!" frequently is an exciting voyage of discovery. Like any journey, there'll be bumps in the road, flat tyres, unexpected diversions and roadblocks along the way. That's just life – I suggest you expect it and have a contingency. Many of us learn by exception and through mistakes: it's a natural way to learn. One of my mottos is "fail fast and often, but never in the same way twice." By that, I mean that getting better and getting larger rewards inevitably means taking greater risk: with greater risk there's a greater chance of rejection or upsetting people. If you're tuned in, you'll learn as much from the times where it doesn't go your way as when it frequently does. Remember that "failure" is only failure when you attach a timescale to it: if it's something that you may try again at some point, then it's actually feedback, not failure.

Making things happen and getting people to work together in a short period of time can be a challenge but I believe the best way of achieving it is to be very open and not hide behind waffle. I have worked on several high-profile business turnarounds over the years and have achieved mobilization of management and colleagues to a common goal by adopting a trusted approach. The steps I have followed are:

- Create the need for change: with a "burning platform" you can establish that the status quo is just not sustainable and that we need to do something different.
- Create a vision or a picture of what the future could be like.
- Have a simple, clear plan to get there with visible ownership of each part of a journey by individuals.
- Make it a series of small steps so people can see they are making progress.
- Make it personal and collective – it is not about "them" it is about "us;" it is not about "him" it is about "me."
- Feed back progress regularly, communicate both individually and collectively and never assume that people know what is going on.
- Celebrate successes no matter how small.

And remember that life changes, so make sure you can adapt your plans to changing circumstances.

By Edward Fitzmaurice, Executive Chairman, Hastings Direct Insurance www.hastingsdirect.com

CHAPTER 16
Good Integrate!

Prepare, Experiment, Refine

So, what's the plan? I invite you to spend a moment thinking about where you'd like to start putting this material into practice. Having a specific activity, meeting or request in mind will help you focus and contextualize your learning. Since it's early days and getting straight to "Yes" is a marathon, not a sprint, I'd encourage you to start small. To be explicit, don't pick the most important negotiation your business has ever seen to try a new technique for the first time – low-risk is better, zero-risk even better yet. Zero-risk means playing with these ideas with your colleagues, friends or family: secretly try out the techniques in a playful way to see just how fabulous some of them are and then ask your audience about their experience of them.

Once you've identified some low-risk scenarios, have a quick scan through the preparation checklist back in Chapter 2 to be clear on your outcomes. Choose your Ask and go forth and "yessify," treating it as an experiment. Experimenting is a useful frame, if you pause to think about it. It means you're purely investigating a hypothesis and, by definition, you can't fail. Instead, you can only learn what happened during and as a result of the experiment. Perhaps it's an investigation that you draw a conclusion from; perhaps you'll experiment with it another time, another place. Afterwards, as any scientist would, spend a minute reflecting on the results or recording your observations: how it went; what worked well; how you'd refine it next time. Then do it again – only better. Following this *prepare, experiment, refine* process is a discipline that will bear fruit when you stick with it. Structured practice is a huge part of success – be patient and be playful.

Masterclass: Become a Layer Player

This book isn't intended to be a one-shot deal, rather a lifelong reference guide for you to come back to every now and again. As you become even more proficient in using these techniques and "feeling" the underpinning science, you'll perhaps start combining multiple approaches into single requests.

You could be the architect of this in at least two ways that I know of: *sequencing* and *stacking*.

1. Sequencing

Imagine two houses side by side: that's the equivalent of sequencing two techniques in time, such as a "Hot coffee, Harvey" (Chapter 14) followed by a "Take-away" (Chapter 12) followed by a "Rejection then retreat" (Chapter 4), to create a snowballing effect.

2. Stacking

Now imagine a block of flats: that's the equivalent of stacking multiple techniques together to use in the same moment to create a bigger initial impact, such as a host of "Body talk" (Chapter 7) with a "Possession is 9/10 of the sale" (Chapter 14) and a "That's not all" (Chapter 4).

I always say the difference between a team achieving 100% and achieving 130% is simple – the team achieving 130% *wants* to do things for you and for each other, rather than *has* to.

Last year, I had to change the go-to-market for one of my teams, which meant a pretty dramatic change in the way we were used to doing things. Rather than getting everyone into a room and taking them through the thought process and the reasons why we needed to change, I opted to get everyone together for a two-day workshop.

On day one, I invited everyone to drill deep into what was and wasn't working in detail, discussing key challenges and their impact. On day two, I framed two exercises. The first was to say, "If we were starting the team from scratch, with a blank piece of paper, what would our team and our go-to-market look like?" Once they had this, the second exercise was, *"How might we get there?"* Because they created the ideal, they did everything in their power to produce a plan of how to get there.

And their plan got us there – a year down the line, our growth is 72% year-on-year. Getting straight to "Yes" is often about giving people the opportunity to convince themselves, rather than you having to convince them.

By John Antunes, Director of SME and Channels,
UK & Ireland at SAP www.sap.com

CHAPTER 17
Some Asks to Avoid

There are definitely certain Asks that I'd like to suggest you avoid like the proverbial plague, since they'll do your results and your relationships no favours. They'll feel attractive and powerful to you as the person making the demand but from the receiver's perspective, reactance will be in full swing. Even if they comply, you're damaging your relationship with them and the potential long-term value you can create together.

1. Emotional Blackmail

Have you ever heard someone say, "If you loved me, you would," or "If you truly were part of this team, you would," or "If you were a kind person, you would," as a device to get their way with you, against your will? It's a trump card and a difficult one to come back from. Yet, how do you feel when this happens? Used? Resentful? Powerless? Your boundaries are almost certainly being violated in this instance. You'll resist internally and either refuse and push back or comply and resent. Neither is a great outcome for the persuader.

It's a fine line and actually shares a strong similarity to "Shared standards" in Chapter 9 of this book. The difference with "Shared standards" is that you raise the standard but put your audience in charge of evaluating the situation and making the decisions. They have control, within the frame that you've set. Emotional blackmail leaves them no room to manoeuvre.

2. Borrowing Authority

In "Authority and insider knowledge" in Chapter 9, I alluded to the fact that frequently using someone else's authority can damage your results potential. "Because Mum said so," "Our CEO says you have to," or, "It's not me asking, you understand, it's a customer in aisle five," all promote the idea that your authority (earned through respect) is insufficient reason for them to act. Instead, you have to pull someone else in to justify action. Beware! Repeated use of this will erode your credibility.

3. Push and Pull Verbs

Something that I'm currently focused on improving in my own communication is my use of push and pull verbs. *Push* verbs communicate our perceived authority over our audience and our rules structure to which we expect them to conform, such as:

- You *need* to
- We *ought* to
- They *have* to
- You *should*
- We *must*
- They've *got* to

Pull verbs, on the other hand, communicate autonomy, potential, respect and freedom for your audience to choose, such as:

- You *might*
- We *can/could*
- You *may*

In practice, this turns:

- "You need to look at this now," into, "You might want to look at this now."
- "You're just going to have to behave in a more mature manner," into, "I know you're able to behave in a more mature manner."
- "Really, your company should take this option," into, "I think your company may find this option most valuable."
- "Your team needs to pay closer attention to the detail going forward," into, "Can I request that your team pays closer attention to the detail going forward?"

It takes a bit of practice but it's worth it. The shift from enforcer to enabler is one that your audience will sense and value. To help you, some handy sentence openers that I appreciate are, "I suggest/My suggestion is . . ." "I'll invite you to . . ." and "Can you/we/they . . . ?" Find a way to articulate such sentiments in your own style, so that it sounds and feels authentic. These convert:

- "You should consider the impact on others," to, "I suggest/My suggestion is that you consider the impact on others."
- "We have to go, now!" to, "Can we go right now?"
- "So, stand up and get into groups, please," to, "So, I'll invite you to stand up and get into groups."

If you remove every single push verb and replace each one with a pull equivalent as you check your written communication, you'll start creating a new habit in your spoken communication without even realizing it. If you find that a challenge, you might consider using the words "perhaps," "possibly," "potentially," or "maybe" before your push verb habits, as a baby step. Perhaps you should try it. The idea of replacing push with pull is that offering someone autonomy is extremely persuasive, counterintuitively.

CHAPTER 18
Making Sure It Sticks

Silence

"Close then shut up!" my first sales manager said to me, "He who speaks first loses!" While my take on business has changed and become collaborative rather than adversarial, there's definitely some truth here. For many people, holding a silence after asking is a challenge: they feel the need to fill up the silence with something, anything – usually talking without purpose. In psychology, it's known as *deflection*: behavior that reduces the perceived awkwardness of the moment.

Silence after asking is important because the person you ask may need to think things over, depending on their decision-making type and the kind of decision type you're asking them to make. Don't interrupt their decision process. A great technique to help you with this is literally to "bite your tongue," a physical barrier to any kind of trivial chatter you may wish to deflect into.

The Three Hungry Diners: Volunteered, Active and Public

A common challenge for executives is that, after an agreement, their audience fails to come good on the deal and follow through. So, perhaps it's useful to spend a few minutes looking at some options here. Using themes from Part One (frames, consistency), Part Two (tribes, herd mentality) and Part Three (brains, reactance) you can now create a robust process to weigh the odds in your favour. The three hungry guests you'd do well to satisfy are *volunteered, active, public*. Once they're fulfilled, your agreements stand a far healthier chance of sticking.

1. Volunteered

In Chapter 12 we explored reactance – the resistance we feel when our boundaries are infringed. Using this principle, it would seem that pulling is better than pushing for the most part. So, after you gain agreement, it makes sense for you to ask your audience to volunteer what *they* think their next steps might be, to move the agreement forward. Importantly, you are asking what they can or will do, not just what you will do – there needs to be some commitment from their side. People are far more likely to stick to something they suggested, rather than something you suggested.

You might ask, "What do you intend to do now, if anything, to move it forward?" or "What do you need to happen next from your side to deliver on this?" or "May I ask what your next action is, to guarantee we hit the deadline?" or "Can we talk next steps? For your part, what will you be doing next to implement this?"

2. Active

A natural extension to this is for them to say or write down what they intend to do. This makes their idea active – it's "out there" in the world, rather than just a passive thought inside their head. Writing things down has a proven link to following through, whether that's on a contract or an email.[1] So, where possible, always hand them the pen or the controls at this point and invite *them* to fill out the form or write the next steps. A signature is also a great way to achieve this: it's a good idea to design a document you'd like them to sign that has a very low perceived risk, unlike a contract, such as a "next steps" document.

Certainly, you could capture agreement in a watertight contract but research shows that stronger written contracts can weaken performance. The twist with weaker contracts is that to get things done in a mutually satisfying way, all parties have to rely on trust.[2]

3. Public

When we've committed to something with other people around, the tribe's presence ramps up our need for consistency dramatically. Consider this: if we welch, we lose not just one person's respect and trust, but the entire tribe's. Therefore, the more public we can make the declaration, the better for us.

Asking who else needs to be brought into the meeting, written to, cc'd in or involved and then immediately updating them on the agreement and next steps holds your audience publicly accountable to their commitments.

Under Promise, Over Deliver

The aim of this book is to offer you strategies that not only improve your results but also your relationships. With this in mind, I hope you always err on the side of caution: be truthful and set realistic expectations for your audience. Trust and loyalty are fragile things in today's world: if you promise things you can't or won't deliver on, your chance of a second chance is negligible.

3 . . . 2 . . . 1 . . .
Commence!

So, that's it. You're ready to go! I hope you've enjoyed the reading and learning experience and that you follow that up with some rewarding practical experiences.

Do you like a deal? Well here's one for you: if you send in your success stories, no matter how small you feel the accomplishment is, to yes@soinflow.com we'll send you a very clever bonus technique PDF of the three missing techniques from this collection (we ran out of room), unavailable anywhere else. If they're particularly great examples, we may even use them in future editions of *Straight to Yes!*

Remember that you didn't learn to walk overnight: you stumbled, banged your head, wobbled and picked yourself back up again. Imagine how different life would be if you'd said, "Forget that! Not worth the effort." Stick with it. Prepare, experiment and refine. Create your own new techniques based on the science. Most of all, enjoy trying new ways of behaving, succeeding and getting straight to "Yes!"

About the Author

Haider "Hedda" Imam is the Founder and Director of the UK business consultancy *So in Flow* and was named UK Sales Trainer of the Year in 2007. Over the last few years, he has worked in close partnership with a rapidly growing roster of national and multinational brands such as Autodesk, EDF Energy, Allied Irish Bank, Merlin Entertainments and more. His passion is helping people in organizations make a genuine difference, whether they're leaders, negotiators or salespeople.

His workshops, programmes and events are innovative, challenging and uplifting: in the last few years, clients have documented more than $74 million ROI that they attribute directly to his collaborations. Clients say that he short-circuits traditional approaches to get rapid results for them.

Haider lives in Newcastle-upon-Tyne, England, with his beautiful wife, Marie-Claire, and their talented teenagers, La'ali and Omar.

Why not Tweet your *Straight to Yes* praise, insights and successes? #s2y

Or join the *Straight to Yes!* community on FaceBook: www.facebook.com/S2Yes

Acknowledgements

To the talented team at *So in Flow*, my friendship: your energy, expertise and coaching inspire me.

To Jonathan and Jenny at Capstone Publishing, my admiration: your laser-like feedback and insight transformed this book.

To Daniel Priestley, my thanks: your eye for a commercial idea is a gift.

To Elizabeth Kuhnke, Kerry Laundon, Claire Rushton and Helen Krag, my appreciation: without you this book may not have found such a good home.

To Professor Patricia Riddell, my gratitude: your expertise and generosity in reviewing the book through a scientific lens is valued.

To Robert Cialdini, Dan Ariely, Daniel Kahneman, Philip Zimbardo and Daniel H. Pink, my respect: your work inspires, fuels and thrills me.

References

Chapter 1 Asking: The "Inner Game"

1. Zhang, T. and Meaney, M. (2010) Epigenetics and the Environmental Regulation of the Genome and Its Function. *Annu. Rev. Psychol.*, *61*, 439–466.
2. Search "Deserving is a Bogus Issue with Mandy Evans" on YouTube.
3. Zhou, X., Zheng, L., Zhou, L. and Guo, N. (2009) The act of rejecting reduces the desire to reconnect: Evidence for a cognitive dissonance account. *J. Experiment. Soc. Psychol.*, *45*(1), 44–50.

Chapter 2 Getting Ready for the Ask

1. Rizzolatti, G. and Sinigaglia, C. (2008) *Mirrors in the Brain. How Our Minds Share Actions and Emotions.* Oxford University Press.
2. Danziger, S., Levav, J. and Avnaim-Pesso, L. (2011) *Extraneous factors in judicial decisions.* PNAS.

Part One Asking with Frames in Mind

1. Levy, B., Hausdorff, J., Hencke, R. and Wei, J. (2000) Reducing cardiovascular stress with positive self-stereotypes of aging. *J. Gerontol. B. Psychol. Sci. Soc. Sci.*, *55*(4), 205–213.

Chapter 3 Consistency

1. Taylor, T. and Booth-Butterfield, S. (1993) Getting a foot in the door with drinking and driving: A field study of healthy influence. *Comm. Res. Rep.*, *10*(1), 95–101.

2. Green, F. (1965) The "foot-in-the-door" technique. *Am. Salesman*, *10*, 14–16.

3. Sherman, S. (1980) On the self-erasing nature of errors of prediction. *J. Personal. Soc. Psychol.*, *39*(2), 211–221.

4. Moriarty, T. (1975) Crime, commitment, and the responsive bystander: Two field experiments. *J. Personal. Soc. Psychol.*, *31*(2), 370–376.

5. Hoover, N. (1999) National Survey: Initiation Rites and Athletics for NCAA Sports Teams.

6. Cialdini, R. and Schroeder, D. (1976) Increasing compliance by legitimizing paltry contributions: When even a penny helps. *J. Personal. Soc. Psychol.*, *34*(4), 599–604.

Chapter 4 Same and Different

1. Tversky, A. and Kahneman, D. (1991) Loss Aversion in Riskless Choice: A Reference Dependent Model. *Quart. J. Econ.*, *106*(4), 1039–1061.

2. Song, H. and Schwarz, N. (2009) If It's Difficult to Pronounce, It Must Be Risky: Fluency, Familiarity, and Risk Perception. *Psychol. Sci.*, *20*(2), 135–138.

3. Alter, A. and Oppenheimer, D. (2006) Predicting short-term stock fluctuations by using processing fluency. *Proc. Nat. Acad. Sci.*, *103*(24), 9369–9372.

4. Cannon, P., Hayes, A. and Tipper, S. (2009) An electromyographic investigation of the impact of task relevance on facial mimicry. *Cognit. Emotion*, *23*(5), 918–929.

5. Cialdini, R., Vincent, J., Lewis, S., Catalan, J., Wheeler, D. and Darby, B. (1975) Reciprocal concessions procedure for inducing compliance: The door-in-the-face technique. *J. Personal. Soc. Psychol.*, *31*(2), 206–215.

6. Burger, J. (1986) Increasing compliance by improving the deal: The that's not all technique. *J. Personal. Soc. Psychol.*, *51*(2), 277–283.

7. Iyengar, S. and Lepper, M. (2000) When choice is demotivating: Can one desire too much of a good thing? *J. Personal. Soc. Psychol.*, *79*(6), 995–1006.

8. Sedikides, C., Ariely, D. and Olsen, N. (1999) Contextual and Procedural Determinants of Partner Selection: On Asymmetric Dominance and Prominance. *Soc. Cogn.*, *17*(2), 118–139.

9. Novemsky, N., Dhar, R., Schwarz, N. and Simonson, I. (2007) Preference Fluency in Choice. *J. Market. Res.*, *44*(3), 347–356.

10. Diemand-Yauman, C., Oppenheimer, D. and Vaughan, E. (2011) Fortune favors the bold (and the italicized): Effects of disfluency on educational outcomes. *Cognition*, *118*(1), 111–115. Epub 2010 Oct 30.

11. Oppenheimer, D. (2006) Consequences of erudite vernacular utilized irrespective of necessity: Problems with using long words needlessly. *Appl. Cogn. Psychol.*, *20*(2), 139–156.

Chapter 5 Ready for Business

1. Yang, S., Kimes, S. and Sessarego, M. (2009) $ or Dollars?: Effects of Menu-price Formats on Customer Price Purchases. *Cornell Hosp. Report*, *9*(8).

Chapter 6 The Way We See It

1. Rosenthal, R. and Jacobson, L. (1992) *Pygmalion in the Classroom* Expanded edition. New York: Irvington.

2. Stinson, D., Cameron, J., Wood, J., Gaucher, D. and Holmes, J. (2009) Deconstructing the "Reign of Error": Interpersonal Warmth Explains the Self-Fulfilling Prophecy of Acceptance. *Personal. Soc. Psychol. Bull.*, *35*, (9) 1165–1178.

3. Peters, W. (1971) *A Class Divided*. New York: Doubleday and Company.

4. Briñol, P., McCaslin, M. and Petty, R. (2012) Self-generated persuasion: Effects of the target and direction of arguments. *J. Personal. Soc. Psychol.*, *102*(5), 925–940.

Part Two Asking with Tribes in Mind

1. Kühn, S., Müller, B., van Baaren, R., Wietzker, A., Dijksterhuis, A. and Brass M. (2010) Why do I like you when you behave like me? Neural mechanisms mediating positive consequences of observing someone being imitated. *Soc. Neurosci.*, *5*(4), 384–392.

2. Bartels, A. and Zeki, S. (2004) The neural correlates of maternal and romantic love. *NeuroImage*, *21*(3), 1155–1166.

Chapter 7 Body Talk

1. Setchell, J., Vaglio, S., Moggi-Cecchi, J., Boscaro, F., Calamai, L. and Knapp, L. (2010) Chemical Composition of Scent-Gland Secretions in an Old World Monkey (*Mandrillus sphinx*): Influence of Sex, Male Status, and Individual Identity. *Chem. Senses*, *35*(3), 205–220.

2. Marzoli, D. and Tommasi, L. (2009) Side biases in humans (*Homo sapiens*): three ecological studies on hemispheric asymmetries. *Naturwissenschaften*, *96*(9), 1099–1106.

3. Berridge, K. and Winkielman, P. (2003) What is an unconscious emotion? (The case for unconscious "liking"). *Cogn. Emotion*, *17*(2),181–211.

4. Tidd, K. and Lockard, J. (1978) Monetary significance of the affiliative smile: A case for reciprocal altruism. *Bull. Psychonom. Soc.*, *11*(6), 344–346.

5. Washburn, P. and Hakel, M. (1973) Visual cues and verbal content as influences on impressions formed after simulated employment interviews. *J. Appl. Psychol.*, *58*(1), 137–141.

6. Forbes, R. and Jackson, P. (1980) Non-verbal behaviour and the outcome of selection interviews. *J. Occup. Psychol.*, *53*(1), 65–72.

7. LaFrance, M. and Hect, M. (1995) Why Smiles Generate Leniency. *Personal. Soc. Psychol Bull.*, *21*(3), 207–214.

8. Strack, F., Martin, L. and Stepper, S. (1988) Inhibiting and facilitating conditions of the human smile: A non-obtrusive test of the facial feedback hypothesis. *J. Personal. Soc. Psychol.*, *54*(5), 768–777.

9. Gueguen, N. and Fischer-Lokou, J. (2003) Tactile Contact and Spontaneous Help: An Evaluation in a Natural Setting. *J. Soc. Psychol.*, *143*(6), 785–787.

10. Levav, J. and Argo, J. (2010) Physical Contact and Financial Risk Taking. *Psychol. Sci.*, *21*(6), 804–810.

11. Hornik, J. (1992) Tactile Stimulation and Consumer Response. *J. Consumer Res.*, *19*(3), 449–458.

12. Robinson, J., Seiter, J. and Acharya, L. (1992) I Just Put My Head Down and Society Does the Rest: An Examination of Influence Strategies Among Beggars. Paper presented to the Western Speech Communication Association, Boise, Idaho.

13. Ernest-Jones, M., Nettle, D. and Bateson, M. (2011) Effects of eye images on everyday cooperative behavior: A field experiment. *Evolution Hum. Behav.*, *32*(3), 172–178.

14. Kellerman, J., Lewis, J. and Laird, J. D. (1989) Looking and loving: The effects of mutual gaze on feelings of romantic love. *J. Res. Personal.*, *23*(2), 145–161.

15. Fry, R. and Smith, G. (1975) The Effects of Feedback and Eye Contact on Performance of a Digit-Coding Task. *J. Soc. Psychol.*, *96*(1), 145–146.

16. Conway, C., Jones, B., DeBruine, L. and Little, A. (2008) Evidence for adaptive design in human gaze preference. *Proc. Roy. Soc. London B*, *275*(1630), 63–69.

17. Hall, E. (1974) *Handbook for Proxemic Research*. Washington D.C.: Society for the Anthropology of Visual Communications.

18. Baron, R. and Bell, P. (1976) Physical Distance and Helping: Some Unexpected Benefits of "Crowding In" on Others. *J. Appl. Soc. Psychol.*, *6*(2), 95–104.

19. Jacob, C. and Guéguen, N. (2012) The Effect of Physical Distance Between Patrons and Servers on Tipping. *J. Hospit. Tourism Res.*, *36*(1), 25–31.

20. Zhong, C. and Leonardelli, G. (2008) Cold and Lonely: Does Social Exclusion Literally Feel Cold? *Psychol. Sci.*, *19*(9), 838–842.

21. Miller, N., Maruyama, G., Beaber, R. and Valone, K. (1976) Speed of speech and persuasion. *J. Personal. Soc. Psychol.*, *34*(4), 615–624.

22. Smith, S. and Shaffer, D. (1995) Speed of Speech and Persuasion: Evidence for Multiple Effects. *Personal. Soc. Psychol. Bull.*, *21*(10), 1051–1060.

Chapter 8 The Name's Bond . . . Social Bond

1. Keysar, B., Converse, B., Wang, J. and Epley, N. (2008) Reciprocity Is Not Give and Take – Asymmetric Reciprocity to Positive and Negative Act. *Psychol. Sci.*, *19*(12), 1280–1286.

2. Falk, A. (2004) Charitable Giving as a Gift Exchange: Evidence from a Field Experiment. Institute of the Study of Labor, Discussion Paper 1148, May.

3. Regan, D. (1971) Effects of a Favor and Liking on Compliance. *J. Experimen. Soc. Psychol.*, *7*, 627–639.
4. Chan, E. and Sengupta, J. (2010) Insincere Flattery Actually Works: A Dual Attitudes Perspective. *J. Market. Res.*, *47*(1), 122–133.
5. Zak, P. J. (2012) *The Moral Molecule: The Source of Love and Prosperity.* Dutton Adult.
6. Li, F. and Miniard, P. (2006) On the Potential for Advertising to Facilitate Trust in the Advertised Brand. *J. Advertising*, *35*(4), 101–112.

Chapter 9 The Wider Tribe

1. Dunbar, R. (1998) *Grooming, Gossip, and the Evolution of Language.* Harvard University Press.
2. Sherif, M., Harvey, O., White, B., Hood, W. and Sherif, C. W. (1961) *The Robbers' Cave Experiment: Intergroup Conflict and Cooperation.* Norman, OK: The University Book Exchange.
3. Darley, J. and Latané, B. (1968) Bystander intervention in emergencies: Diffusion of responsibility. *J. Personal. Soc. Psychol.*, *8*(4 Pt 1), 377–383.
4. Diamond, S. (2012) *Getting More: How to Negotiate to Achieve Your Goals in the Real World.* Three Rivers Press.
5. Milgram, S. (1963) Behavioral Study of Obedience. *J. Abnormal Soc. Psychol.*, *67*(4), 371–378.
6. Haney, C., Banks, W. C. and Zimbardo, P. G. (1973) Interpersonal Dynamics in a Simulated Prison. *Int. J. Criminol. Penol.*, *1*, 69–97.

Chapter 10 Progressive Feedback Loops

1. van Baaren, R., Holland, R., Steenaert, B. and van Knippenberg, A. (2003) Mimicry for money: Behavioral consequences of imitation. *J. Experimen. Soc. Psychol.*, *39*(4), 393–398.
2. Leander, N., Chartrand, T. and Bargh, J. (2012) You Give Me the Chills: Embodied Reactions to Inappropriate Amounts of Behavioral Mimicry. *Psychol. Sci.*, *23*(7), 772–779.
3. Chartrand, T. and Bargh, J. (1999) The chameleon effect: The perception-behavior link and social interaction. *J. Personal. Soc. Psychol.*, *76*(6), 893–910.

4. van Baaren, R., Holland, R., Kawakami, K. and van Knippenberg, A. (2004) Mimicry and Prosocial Behavior. *Psychol. Sci.*, *15*(1), 71–74.
5. Brinol, P. and Petty, R. (2003) Overt head movements and persuasion: A self-validation analysis. *J. Personal. Soc. Psychol.*, *84*(6), 1123–1139.

Part Three Asking with the Brain in Mind

Chapter 11 The Loss and Pain Brain

1. Tversky, A. and Kahneman, D. (1981) The framing of decisions and the psychology of choice. *Science*, *211*(4481), 453–458.
2. Weller, J., Levin, I., Shiv, B. and Bechara, A. (2007) Neural Correlates of Adaptive Decision Making for Risky Gains and Losses. *Psychol. Sci.*, *18*(11), 958–964.
3. Buchel, C. and Dolan, R. (2000) Classical fear conditioning in functional neuroimaging. *Curr. Opin. Neurobiol.*, *10*(2), 219–223.
4. Lieberman, M. and Eisenberger, N. (2009) Pains and Pleasures of Social Life. *Science*, *32*(5916), 890–891.
5. Kalichman, S. and Coley, B. (1995) Context framing to enhance HIV-antibody-testing messages targeted to African American women. *Health Psychol.*, *14*(3), 247–254.
6. Rothman, A. and Salovey, P. (1997) Shaping perceptions to motivate healthy behavior: The role of message framing. *Psychol. Bull.*, *121*(1), 3–19.
7. Meyerowitz, B. and Chaiken, S. (1987) The effect of message framing on breast self-examination attitudes, intentions, and behavior. *J. Personal. Soc. Psychol.*, *52*(3), 500–510.
8. Chatterjee, P. and Rose, R. (2012) Do Payment Mechanisms Change the Way Consumers Perceive Products? *J. Cons. Res.*, *38*(6), 1129–1139.
9. Kahneman, D., Knetsch, J. and Thaler, R. (1991) Anomalies: The Endowment Effect, Loss Aversion, and Status Quo Bias. *J. Econ. Pers.*, *5*(1), 193–206.

Chapter 12 Reactance

1. Brehm, J. (1966) *A Theory of Psychological Reactance*. Academic Press.

Chapter 13 Pattern Breakers

1. Santos, M., Leve C. and Pratkanis, A. (1994) Hey Buddy, Can You Spare Seventeen Cents? Mindful Persuasion and the Pique Technique. *J. Appl. Soc. Psychol.*, *29*(9), 755–764.
2. Davis, B. and Knowles, E. (1999) A disrupt-then-reframe technique of social influence. *J. Personal. Soc. Psychol.*, *76*(2), 192–199.
3. Langer, E., Blank, A. and Chanowitz, B. (1978) The mindlessness of ostensibly thoughtful action: The role of "placebic" information in interpersonal interaction. *J. Personal. Soc. Psychol.*, *36*(6), 635–642.
4. Boster, F., Shaw, A., Hughes, M., Kotowski, M., Strom, R. and Deatrick, L.(2009) Dump-and-Chase: The Effectiveness of Persistence as a Sequential Request Compliance – Gaining Strategy. *Comm. Stud.*, *60*(3), 219–234.
5. Beaman, A., Klentz, B., Diener, E. and Svanum, S. (1979) Self-awareness and transgression in children: Two field studies. *J. Personal. Soc. Psychol.*, *37*(10), 1835–1846.

Chapter 14 Priming

1. *Derren Brown: Mind Control. "Animal Heaven"* (Series 4, episode 1). Objective Productions/Channel 4.
2. Meyers-Levy, J. and Zhu, J. (2007) The Influence of Ceiling Height: The Effect of Priming on the Type of Processing That People Use. *J. Cons. Res.*, *34*(2), 174–186.
3. Fitzsimons, G. M., Chartrand, T. and Fitzsimons, G. J. (2008) Automatic Effects of Brand Exposure on Motivated Behavior: How Apple Makes You "Think Different." *J. Cons. Res.*, *35*(1), 21–35.
4. Liu, J. E., Smeesters, D. and Trampe, D. (2012) Effects of Messiness on Preferences for Simplicity. *J. Cons. Res.*, *39*(1), 199–214.
5. Kay, A., Wheeler, S., Bargh, J. and Ross, L. (2004) Material priming: the influence of mundane physical objects on situational construal and competitive behavioral choice. *Org. Behav. Hum. Decision Proc.*, *95*(1), 83–96.

6. Sanna, L., Chang, E., Miceli, P. and Lundberg, K. (2011) Rising up to higher virtues: Experiencing elevated physical height uplifts prosocial actions. *J. Experimen. Soc. Psychol.*, *47*(2), 472–476.

7. Williams, L. and Bargh, J. (2008) Experiencing Physical Warmth Promotes Interpersonal Warmth. *Science*, *322*(5901), 606–607.

8. Martin, P., Laing, J., Martin, R. and Mitchell, M. (2005) Caffeine, cognition, and persuasion: Evidence for caffeine increasing the systematic processing of persuasive messages. *J. Appl. Soc. Psychol.*, *35*(1), 160–182.

9. Ackerman, M., Nocera, C. and Bargh, J. (2010) Incidental Haptic Sensations Influence Social Judgments and Decisions. *Science*, *328*(5986), 1712–1715.

10. Piqueras-Fiszman, B. and Spence, C. (2011) Does the weight of the dish influence our perception of food? *Food Qual. Pref.*, *22*(8), 753–756.

11. Piqueras-Fiszman, B. and Spence, C. (2012) The weight of the bottle as a possible extrinsic cue with which to estimate the price (and quality) of the wine? Observed correlations. *Food Qual. Pref.*, *25*(1), 41–45.

12. Holland, R., Hendriks, M. and Aarts, H. (2005) Smells like Clean Spirit: Nonconscious Effects of Scent on Cognition and Behavior. *Psychol. Sci.*, *16*(9), 689–693.

13. Peck, J. and Shu. S. (2009) The Effect of Mere Touch on Perceived Ownership. *J. Cons. Res.*, *36*(3), 434–447.

14. *Star Trek: First Contact* (1996) Paramount Pictures.

Part Four Commencement

Chapter 18 Making Sure It Sticks

1. Cioffi, D. and Garner, R. (1996) On Doing the Decision: Effects of Active versus Passive Choice on Commitment and Self-Perception. *Personal. Soc. Psychol. Bull.*, *22*(2), 133–147.

2. Bohnet, I., Frey, B. and Huck, S. (2000) More Order with Less Law: On Contract Enforcement, Trust, and Crowding. *Am. Politic. Sci. Rev.*, *95*(1), 131–144.

Index

accents 100–1
Acceptance Prophecy 81
Action Comics 150
active 208–9
add-on sell 41
"aesthetic enjoyment"
    experiment 108–9
affiliation 123–4
ageing stereotypes 34
alternative choice 74–5
altruism 149
Amazon 155–6
American Cancer Research
    Society 41–2, 45
amygdala 144, 148
anchors, bias and contast 58
Antunes, John 201
Apple 50, 150
"Apply to Buy" 44–5
approach 190
Argos 153
Ariely, Dan 58, 60, 153
Asda 93
Ask checklist 21–6
Ask, suitability of 26–7
assumptive ask 73–4
attractiveness, comparisons in
    60–1

authority 27, 126–7
    borrowing 204
Avaaz.org 122
avoidance behaviours 190

Baaren, Rick van 88
baby boomers 2
Bargh, J. 186
barrier to action 46, 47
bartering 52–3
Bateson, Melissa 97
Beaman, Arthur 174
Bennett, Drake 49
Berkshire Hathaway 99
Berridge, K. 94
Blair, Paul 38
Blank, A. 171
blueprint of life 17
body language 91–103
bonding 105–17
brain 144–5, 147–8
    amygdala 144, 148
    pre-frontal cortex (PFC)
        25–6, 169
Brown, Derren 179, 180
Buffett, Warren 99
Burger, J. 55–6
buy-in, creating 3

INDEX

buy now, pay later 153–4
buying signal 68–9
  leveraging 71–3
bystander effect 122

Carter, Jimmy 113
celebrity 124
chairs 185–6
chameleon effect 88
Chan, Elaine 112
Chanowitz, B. 171
Children in Need 149
choice architecture 159
choices: gold, silver, bronze
    57–60
Cialdini, Robert 42, 151
Coca-Cola 112, 158
cognitive dissonance 40
Comet 153
Comic Relief 149
commitment 42
communication 23
complexity 50–1
conditional requesting 68–9,
    86
connection 88, 105
consensus 121
consent, presumed 158–9
Consignia 158
consistency 37–48
consistency two-step 39–40,
    42–3, 47
contact, physical 95–7
contingency contracts 70–1,
    86
cross sell 41

Darwin, Charles 12
deadlines 23
decision making
    brain and 148
    "gut instincts" in 28
    time of day and 26
defaults rule 158–9
deflection 207
deserving, concept of 15
Diamond, Stuart 128
diffusion of responsibility 122
Disney Vacations 110
disrupt then reframe (DTR)
    171
door-in-the-face technique
    52–4
dopamine 149
dump and chase (DAC) 172–4
Dunbar, Robin 119

ear dominance 91–3
ego depletion 179
elevation 181–3
Elliot, Jane 81
emotional blackmail 203–4
emotional/physical state
    24–5
endorphins 183
Enfield, Harry 161
environment 25–6, 180–2
ethics 9
Evans, Mandy 15
eye contact 97–8

Facebook 2, 4, 123, 124
facial feedback 95

INDEX

failure to thrive syndrome 105
familiar contrast 50–1
familiarity 49–50
fear of discomfort 18
fear of failure 15
fear of rejection 15–16
fear of success 16–17
fight or flight behaviours 161
fine-tuning 196–7
Fitzmaurice, Edward 198
flattery 112–13
"flip the bennies" 151–2
fonts 62
foot-in-the-door 40–2
forbidden fruit 165–6, 190
Ford, Henry 18
frames of reference 34–5
freedom shopping 56–7
Fry, R. 97

Galton, Francis 12
Gandhi, Mahatma 115
Generation Y (Millenials) 2
Gigerenzer, Gerd 28
Gilley, Jeremy 175
Ginnelly, Margaret 6
Godin, Seth 17
Google+ 124
"gut instincts" 28

handshake 99–100
Hare, Kimberley 90
Hartunian, Paul 55
Hatson, Matt 80
hazing 44
herd mentality 121–3

heuristics 26, 28
honesty 174–5
Hoover, Dr Nadine C. 44
Hornik, Jacob 96–7
Howard, Daniel 42
humility 114–15
Hutchinson, Clive 162
hypnotic nod 135
hypothetical frames 83

Imam-Gutierrez, Omar 10
inconsistency 37
inhibition 29
inhibitors 14–19
    deserving 15
    fear of discomfort 18
    fear of rejection 15–16
    fear of success 16–17
    wrong peer group 18–19
initiation rituals 44
insider knowledge 126–7
iTunes 124
Iyengar, Sheena 59

Jehovah's Witnesses 41
job loyalty 2
Jobs, Steve 50
Jones, Steve 12–13

Kahneman, Daniel 179
Kay. A. 181
Kellerman, J. 97
Kimes, Dr Sheryl E. 76
King, Martin Luther
    102
Knowles, Eric 171

INDEX

Langer, E. 171
Laird, J.D. 97
leadership, demonstrate
    130–1
leveraging buying signals 71–3
Lewis, J. 97
libertarian paternalism 159
limited editions 150–1
LinkedIn 45
Littlewoods 153

magnetic middle (herd
    mentality) 121–3
Marriott, Steve 20
Marzoli, Daniele 92
mass influence 184–5
McKenna, Paul 14
McLane Distribution 99
Mehrabian, Albert 91
memes 182
Mere Exposure Effect 49
micro-financing 2
Microsoft 180
Milgram, Stanley 130
mimicry 88–9, 133–4
mindfulness 171–2
mismatching 164–5

nature vs. nurture 12–13
negotiation 24
Neill, Michael 14
nervousness 24–5
neuro-linguistic programming
    (NLP) 135–6
neuromarketing 2, 149

Obama, Barack 101, 159
O'Bannon, Dan 49
obligation 110–11
one-click authorization 155–6
Operation Momentum 97
organ donation 158–9
ownership, touch and 187–9
oxytocin 113–14, 183

paltry requests 45–7
Papps, Rob 66
pattern blindness 83
pattern breakers 169–77
Peck, Joann 188
peer group, wrong 18–19
perceptual contrast 53–4, 57–8
"PerfectStore" mailshot 112–13
personal data mining 105
personalization 105
persuasive sentence openers and
    closers 137–9
Peston, Robert 126
physical contact 95–7
piquing 169–70
point of view of others 23–4
polar asking 164–5
porgressive feedback loops
    133–41
Power Analysis 67
power of "Yes" 134–6
pre-frontal cortex (PFC) 25–6,
    169
prepare, experiment, refine
    process 199–200
present bias 153

INDEX

price comparisons 75–7
priming 179–90
pro-social behaviour 45
proxemics 98–9
psychological reactance 128, 161–7
public 209
pull verbs 204–5
purpose 22
push verbs 204–5
Pygmalion effect 79–81, 86

rapport 88
rarities 150–1
reactance 161–7, 190
readiness 196
reciprocity 9, 53, 55, 107
Reed, Richard 31
refusal script 170
Regan, Dennis 108
rejection then retreatment 52–4
relationships, building 28–9
requests as opportunities 65–8
resources, fight for 3–4
response potential 165–6
responsiveness 27–8
Results Corporation plc 28–9
rhymes 61–2
risk-taking 24
Rizzolatti, G. 25
"Robber's Cave" experiment 119
Robbins, Tony 19
Ross, L. 181
Rowland, Robin 106

Royal Mail 158
rules of thumb 26

sacrifice 24
Sade, Marquis de 165
Sanna, Larry 182
self-interest 24
self-perception 37, 41–2
self-persuasion 81–2
self-promotion 114–16
Sengupta, Jaideep 112
sequencing 200
serotonin 13, 183
seven meeting rule 106
"shared standard" 127–9
sharp angle 68–9
sheep factor 121
Sherif, Muzafer 119
Sherman, Steven J. 41
Shu, Suzanne 188
Shusett, Ronald 49
simplification 50–1
Smart, Jamie 56
SmileyWorld 93
smiling 93–5
Smith, G. 97
"smooth talking" 101–2
social bonds 105–17
social inhibition 29
social networking 2, 105
social proof 121–3
social taboo 125–6
Sony PlayStation 147–8
Sophos 110
speech, speed of 102

INDEX

Sport Relief 149
Spotify 124, 157–8
"squeeze page", website 41
stacking 200
standards, shared 127–9
state dependence of behaviour 25
Stobart, Paul 120
survival of the fittest 182

T-Mobile 50
take-away 163
tend and befriend 161
Tesco 153
that's not all (TNA) technique 54–6
Three Mobile 50
tidiness 186–7
time as resource 4–5
timescales 23
timing of request 25–6
Tommasi, Dr Luca 92
touch, ownership and 187–9
Toys "R" Us 147
trial basis 157–8
TripAdvisor 122
trust 106, 113–14, 183
Twitter 2, 4
Tyson, Mike 154

ugly twin 60–1
unconscious emotion 94
undesired option 51–2
UNICEF 176
United Nations 175
universals 136

Very.co.uk 153
vice 152–3
virtue 152–3
Vistaprint 41
vocal pitch 100–1
volunteered 208

Wal-Mart 93, 99
warmth 183–4
Watzlawick, Paul 56
WHO 176
Wikipedia 122, 126–7
Winkielman, P. 94
World Peace Day 175

YouTube 122

Zajonc, Robert 49
Zak, Paul 113–14
Zimbardo, Philip 130
Zumba 122

Index compiled by Annette Musker